Cloyce Box

6'4" and Bulletproof

SWAIM-PAUP-FORAN SPIRIT OF SPORT SERIES

Sponsored by James C. '74 & Debra Parchman Swaim,
Nancy & T. Edgar Paup '74, and Joseph Wm. & Nancy Foran

Cloyce Box

6'4" and Bulletproof

Michael Barr

Texas A&M University Press
COLLEGE STATION

First edition

This paper meets the requirements of ANSI/NISO Z39.48–1992 (Permanence of Paper).
Binding materials have been chosen for durability.
Manufactured in the United States of America

Library of Congress Cataloging-in-Publication Data

Names: Barr, Michael D., 1952– author.
Title: Cloyce Box, 6'4" and bulletproof / Michael Barr.
Other titles: Swaim-Paup-Foran spirit of sport series.
Description: First edition. | College Station : Texas A&M University Press, [2017] | Series: Swaim-Paup-Foran spirit of sport series | Includes bibliographical references and index.
Identifiers: LCCN 2017017733 | ISBN 9781623495763 (book/cloth : alk. paper) |
ISBN 9781623495770 (ebook)
Subjects: LCSH: Box, Cloyce, 1923–1993. | Football players—United States—Biography. | Businessmen—United States—Biography.
Classification: LCC GV939. B673 B37 2017 | DDC 796.332092 [B]—dc23 LC record available at https://lccn.loc.gov/2017017733

Cover and title page photo courtesy AP Photo/Art Everett

This book is dedicated to the people of Jonesboro, Texas.
They take care of each other.

A

I denied myself nothing my eyes desired:
I refused my heart no pleasure.
My heart took delight in all my labor,
and this was the reward for all my toil.
Yet when I surveyed all that my hands had done
and what I had toiled to achieve,
everything was meaningless, a chasing after the wind,
nothing was gained under the sun.

—Ecclesiastes 2:10–11, Attributed to King Solomon

Contents

A gallery of images follows page 79.

Acknowledgments

Cloyce Box was a powerful and controversial figure. Even now, almost twenty-five years after his death, some people who knew him refused to talk about him. To those men and women who chose to share their thoughts and memories with me on the record, I thank you.

Photographs that appear in this book were made available to me through the combined efforts of Gary Adams, Adams Affiliates, Inc.; Susie Self, AGN Media; Garet von Netzer, former publisher of the *Amarillo Globe-News*; Matt Dossey, ISD Superintendent; and the staff at the Special Collections Unit, Cornette Library, West Texas A&M University. Thanks to you all.

Cloyce Box

6'4" and Bulletproof

Introduction

As the ring of lights above Soldier Field bore down on the playing surface with a radiance that outshone the Chicago skyline, Frank Gifford, high in the booth with Al Michaels and Dan Dierdorf, announced to a nationwide audience watching *Monday Night Football* that Cloyce Box had died. The news was meaningless to most viewers who had just settled in to watch the Vikings and the Bears square off on week eight of the 1993 season. The average football fan could hardly be expected to remember a man who hadn't taken the field in almost forty years. But, to an elite group of former athletes, celebrities, politicians, business executives, and Wall Street heavyweights, the news was heard and noted.

Three days later a who's who of sports, entertainment, and business attended a memorial service for Box at Lovers Lane United Methodist Church in Dallas, Texas. Cloyce and his first wife Fern were long-time members of that congregation at 9200 Inwood Road. In happier times, Fern, the daughter of a Methodist minister, played the piano there and sang in the choir.

At the service, Hall of Fame running back Doak Walker sat near the front of the church, just behind the family. Carol Layne, Bobby Layne's widow, sat nearby with a royal delegation of Box's teammates from the old Detroit Lions glory days including Yale Lary, Harley Sewell, Jim David, Thurman McGraw, Jim Neal, and Leon Hart. Writer, journalist, and Kennedy assassination expert Hugh Aynesworth came to the service to pay respects to his old friend and former boss.

Honorary pallbearers included Frank Gifford, former Kentucky governor and former CEO of Kentucky Fried Chicken John Y. Brown Jr., former CEO of Mercantile National Bank Dallas Gene Bishop, and chairman of the board and CEO of Lincoln Properties Mack Pogue. Sitting next to Governor Brown was his wife, former Miss America and TV personality Phyllis George.

Important people with less familiar faces filled the remaining pews. The men dressed in expensive suits, the women in designer dresses with skin as taut as a strand of barbed wire.

The memorial service, like Box's life, was carefully planned, rehearsed, and executed. After an opening prayer, wealthy Highland Park philanthropist and socialite Dianne Cash sang "Amazing Grace." Frank Gifford delivered the eulogy. Frank's wife, TV personality and recording artist Kathie Lee Gifford, sang "He Giveth More Grace." Two days earlier, an audience of millions heard Mrs. Gifford pay a tearful tribute to Cloyce Box on her daytime television show *Regis and Kathie Lee.*

Box's son Doug said it best: "It was like the pope had died."

Who was this man, mourned by the rich and famous but unknown to the rest of the world?

Cloyce Box was an American original. He was handsome, athletic, intelligent, and ambitious, and his life was the stuff of which dreams and miniseries are made. He was a dirt-poor farm boy from the Texas backcountry who used his great talents to become a star in the National Football League, a corporate CEO, and a very wealthy man. He was fearless, flamboyant, and controversial, and his story is an epic Texas tale of football, cattle, horses, oil, money, power, incredible success, and magnificent failure.

He rubbed elbows with US presidents, coddled South American dictators, and counted as his friends and partners the blue bloods and billionaires of American society. He did business with the Rockefellers. He shared cocktails at the Kentucky Derby with Donald Trump. Hillary Clinton owned stock in his company. He borrowed millions from Trammell Crow with a phone call. He owned a Learjet, a Florida horse farm, an apartment on New York's Upper East Side, and a Texas ranch that was the first home of the TV show *Dallas*, but any similarities between Cloyce Box and J. R. Ewing are purely coincidental.

Then again, maybe not.

1

A Wide Spot in the Road

Life is either a daring adventure or nothing.

—Helen Keller

An extraordinary life began for Cloyce Kennedy Box, and his twin brother Boyce Murrell Box, on a hot August afternoon in the back room of a clapboard shack near the community of Plainview in Coryell County, Texas. When the Box twins came into this world in 1923, there was no doctor to help with the delivery and no birth certificate—not an unusual situation for families in this part of the country. In the 1920s, a hospital birth was more the exception than the rule in rural Coryell County, and the blessed event was more likely recorded on the pages of the family Bible than on a birth certificate at the courthouse.

Fifteen years later, on the testimony of two women present at their birth, the Texas Department of Health issued birth certificates for Cloyce and Boyce Box, probably to help them get government benefits as indigent children. The Box twins were bona fide.

Cloyce's paternal grandparents, Robert D. Box, Sr. and Eliza Jane Clark Box, came to Central Texas in the 1880s from Gilmer in East Texas in a horse-drawn wagon, bound for Gatesville on the edge of the rolling hill country.

As the wagon carrying R. D. and Eliza Box approached Gatesville, a steam whistle from a Cotton Belt Railroad locomotive spooked the team and caused a runaway. Although it appeared that everyone survived the incident without injury, R. D. had concerns about Eliza who was pregnant at the time.

A whistle-chasing lawyer from Waco read about the runaway in the local newspaper and offered his services to sue the railroad. R. D. agreed, but soon after the lawsuit began, the two parties settled out of court with the railroad consenting to pay the plaintiffs a certain amount of cash rather than trust the case to a lengthy and expensive trial. With the money, R. D. and Eliza built a two-story house on a small farm between the communities of Plainview and King, just west of Gatesville, near the banks of Cowhouse Creek.[1]

Cloyce was fascinated by the story of the shyster lawyer from Waco with the power to extract money from the almighty railroad. It inspired him to become an attorney.

Cloyce's father, Robert D. Box Jr., was born on the family farm at Plainview on November 2, 1891. R. D. worked the farm alongside his father until he joined the army in 1917. After basic training, his unit shipped to France as part of the American Expeditionary Forces.

R. D. Jr was a patriot, but he struggled in the military. His health was not robust. He suffered from asthma and other ailments.[2] He was also a sensitive and vulnerable young recruit who never adjusted to army life. Although he saw no action on the battlefield, he was lonely in France, homesick for his family back in Texas. He returned to Plainview in 1919 without visible scars, but suffered severe bouts of depression-like symptoms the rest of his life. His invisible wounds would have terrible consequences for Cloyce and his family.

On December 20, 1920, R. D. Jr. married Zelma Ray Carter. The young couple had four children: Sybil Janice, Cloyce Kennedy, Boyce Murrell, and Wilmuth Mavinee.

For ten years, R. D. Jr. and Zelma helped farm the home place at Plainview; then in 1930, they bought a farm of their own near Jonesboro, 20 miles to the north along the Coryell and Hamilton County line. Later they bought another small farm on a rocky hill they called "the mountain place."

The Box children did most of their growing up in Jonesboro—a tiny unincorporated village that sits on a low hill 50 miles west of Waco. They attended school in Jonesboro and fell under the influence of the remarkable people of that small community. Cloyce

Box became a famous professional athlete and a rich and powerful man, but he thought of Jonesboro every day of his life.

Jonesboro is located on the edge of West Texas. Besides the rolling hills and cedar brakes, the Leon River is the most significant geographical feature of the countryside. The river forms an irregular semicircle just west of town. The Leon is a sluggish, winding stream with steep banks and gravel shoals separated by pools of dark, murky water.

Much of the soil in this part of Texas is thin, rocky, and harder than reinforced concrete, but centuries of flooding along the Leon have gouged a narrow valley and filled it with deep fertile soil. The Leon River is no thing of beauty, but its bottomland is some of the most productive farmland on earth.

In a very real way, the river determines the social pattern in this farming community. Bottomland is more productive and more valuable than land away from the river. Bottomland farmers produce more crops and make more money. Away from the river, yields are smaller and a dollar is a lot harder to come by. Cloyce Box was raised on a rocky hill, but spent his life in headlong pursuit of bottomland.

The people of Jonesboro, the river, and the rough countryside molded the lives of Cloyce and Boyce Box as surely as floodwaters made the Leon River valley. Although the Box brothers left Jonesboro at an early age, made fortunes, and traveled the world, they never escaped the influence of that rugged country or the people who looked after them and cared for them when they were young. They always carried a tender spot in their hearts for the people of this small Texas town, and the lessons they learned in Jonesboro stayed with them the rest of their lives.

To most travelers, Jonesboro was nothing more than a wide spot in the road between Hamilton and Gatesville, but it was a special place to the people who called it home. The town was literally born of the river when brothers William and David Jones built a sawmill on the Leon in 1866. By the turn of the twentieth century, Jonesboro boasted a general store (owned by Mr. Rankin), a gristmill, a sawmill, a steam-powered cotton gin, a school, a post office, and two churches.

But unlike most towns, Jonesboro has changed little in size and appearance in the last one hundred years. Today there are maybe thirty modest buildings in the town proper, including a public school; a combination convenience store, café, and gas station; a post office; a community center; two churches (Baptist and Methodist); and a vacant restaurant, all clustered along State Highway 36, FM 1602 and 217, and four county roads. Today, Jonesboro has that look of a small town that is holding on for the present, but with no ironclad guarantees for the future.

Counting the homesteads in a 10-mile radius, maybe 300 people lived in greater Jonesboro when Cloyce and Boyce Box grew up there in the 1930s. On a good day, if the cotton was picked, the farm chores done, and the catfish weren't biting down on the Leon, about one hundred students attended the two-story red brick building that housed the Jonesboro public school. The school was, and remains to this day, the pride of the town, the heart and soul of the community, and the symbol of hope for tomorrow. When the future of Jonesboro looked grim and uncertain, the school held the community together.

That future seemed secure in the first decade of the twentieth century when the Stephenville North and South Texas Railroad announced it would lay track from Stephenville to Gatesville by way of Hamilton, but engineers chose a route that bypassed Jonesboro, going instead to the west through Levita, Ireland, and Aleman, the grade being more favorable in that direction. Those communities prospered, briefly, while Jonesboro lost some of its vitality.

The railroad normally guaranteed growth and prosperity to western towns along its path, but times and the economy were changing. By the start of World War II, cars, trucks, good roads, and cheap gasoline had put many of the rural rail lines out of business. The small Central Texas towns that sprang up along the rails dried up. Today, Levita, Ireland, and Aleman are ghost towns, while Jonesboro, located along a major highway, is alive and kicking.

Jonesboro is the kind of close-knit, cohesive community that is rare today but was common in rural Texas in the early twentieth century. A relatively small number of families owned the land around Jonesboro, and many of those families were connected by marriage.

A man learned early on to stick by his family through thick and thin because the family was his protection against threats from the outside. Families survived by sticking together. Kin folks could disagree among themselves and even come to blows without tearing the family apart, but serious conflicts between families or with outsiders sometimes led to feuding and bloodshed.

When a dispute arose, the nearest lawman was too far away to do any good. The families of Jonesboro had a tradition of taking such matters into their own hands.

Cloyce Box grew to manhood in a society governed by a strict rural code. Boys learned manliness and independence at an early age. Girls were watched and protected. The toughest boys rose to the top of the adolescent pecking order. Being tough was more important than being smart, even if toughness occasionally spilled over into brutality.

Country people admired strength and courage above all else. A real man never admitted mistakes, backed down, or showed weakness. He stood his ground whatever the cost. A real man was aggressive, because an aggressive man got his way. A real man ruled his family with an iron hand. His orders were not disputed or even questioned.

The people of Jonesboro were reserved in a way the modern world of Facebook and Twitter cannot understand. Family business was a private matter and never discussed in public. People celebrated and grieved in private. Society frowned on flashy or pretentious behavior. People, especially men, were not demonstrative. They kept their feelings to themselves.

The culture produced a people that were strong, self-reliant, and militantly independent. They had to be. They feared God and little else. They didn't need the sheriff for protection or the government for assistance during hard times. Family members supported each other and helped each other through difficult circumstances.

But at the same time, the closeness could be stifling and uncomfortable. There were no strangers in Jonesboro and no secrets. Gossip and rumor traveled along the grapevine at warp speed. Everyone knew about the Baptist deacon who beat his wife and the promiscuous teenage girl suddenly sent away to live with relatives in Waco or Dallas. Everybody counted the number of months between a young couple's wedding day and the birth of their first child.

When the Box brothers were young, this part of the country was still relatively new to settlement, just a couple of generations removed from the pioneers. The people still displayed the toughness and the grim self-reliance of the men and women who first tamed this part of Texas with guns, plows, and Bibles.

The isolation and difficulties of life produced a bedrock conservatism that made the people intensely patriotic but highly suspicious of government. Racism was a familiar part of the rural southern culture. *Yankee* was still a bad word in Jonesboro. The Wild West was a recent memory. Comanches roamed this land less than 50 years before. They made camp all along the Leon. Their stone artifacts are still scattered along its banks.

The spring and fall are the most pleasant times of the year in this part of the world, although each of those seasons lasts but a short time. The winter is usually damp and cold while the long Texas summer is bone dry and hotter than nine kinds of hell.

The country philosophers who drink coffee every morning at the One Stop Convenience Store and Cafe at the corner of Highway 36 and FM 217 say that when Satan was expelled from heaven, he stopped awhile in Jonesboro to get acclimated to his new home. They say that when Noah built the ark and the rain fell 40 days and nights, Jonesboro got a half-inch.

Jonesboro in the 1920s and 30s was a quieter place than it is today; before the rattle and hum of engine-driven machinery and the constant roar of cars and trucks barreling through town on Highway 36 (named for the Texas 36th Division of World War II fame). In the old days, farmers shouted back and forth to each other across distant fields. Many of the old timers clearly remember the first time they heard the train whistle off to the west, and the memory excites them to this day. It was the first mechanized sound they had ever heard.

The nights before electricity were unimaginably dark and silent. Even a gentle breeze carried sounds of the night great distances. A boy lying still in his bed could easily hear a dog bark, a calf bawl, or a screen door slam a half-mile away. Nights were so dark, the only light came from the moon and stars; so still, the only sound was the beat of one's own heart.

But all that was about to change—thanks to Mr. Roosevelt and the New Deal. The McLennan County Electric Cooperative, organized with a loan from the Rural Electrification Administration, began electrifying rural parts of Central Texas in 1935. Jonesboro received its first jolt of electricity on November 29, 1939.

But the Box family continued to live in darkness. They could not afford the $25 hookup charge or the $2.25 minimum monthly fee—also known as the "light bill."

Travel in any direction in that part of Texas was difficult in the 1920s and 30s. Few people had cars. The main roads were poorly maintained, and the others were not maintained at all. As late as 1935, there were few bridges and not an inch of pavement in all of Coryell County.

Then in the 1930s, Texas acquired the right of way through the center of the state for a proposed highway from Abilene to the gulf coast. In Central Texas, the route generally followed the old military supply road along the western frontier between Fort Gates in Coryell County and Fort Phantom Hill just north of Abilene. That road, and highway that followed, ran right through the middle of Jonesboro.

Paving on the new road began in 1935 but didn't reach Coryell County until several years after the war. In 1935, the road that would become State Highway 36 was a surfaced road topped with a thin layer of caliche. The road between Gatesville and Waco, the road that would become US Highway 84, was nothing more than graded earth that turned into black waxy goo after a thunderstorm. The road between Gatesville and Temple was an unmaintained wagon path from Gatesville to The Grove on the Bell County Line.[3]

Just getting from one place to another was so difficult that most people never tried. Before World War II, the difficulties of travel were such that most of the men and women who lived in the low chalky hills and cedar brakes around Jonesboro were born there and would die there with only a simple stone marker in the Jonesboro Cemetery to note their passing. Only a persistent, adventurous, and lucky few found a way out.

Yet, seventeen miles down the dusty road was another world. Gatesville was no metropolis, but compared to Jonesboro, it was downright exotic and cosmopolitan. It had a movie theater, a soda shop, a skating rink, a hospital, two banks, several doctors, a dentist, a weekly newspaper, a jail, and a majestic limestone courthouse with three stories and a basement. A traveler could hop a train at the depot on the east end of town and after changing trains in Waco, ride all the way to Galveston.

On a single Saturday afternoon, there was more activity on the square in Gatesville than Jonesboro saw in a year. Black people lived in Gatesville—and Catholics. There was a rumor that some people in Gatesville voted Republican.

Hayden "Hayboy" Young, Cloyce Box's childhood friend recalled that "Life was simpler then. Not too many choices. In the early fall we picked cotton five days a week and til noon on Saturday. School didn't start until late September. On Saturday afternoon we went swimming in the Leon River or went to a movie at the Ritz Theater on the south side of the square in Gatesville. Other than that we didn't get too far away from home. Today people go to Dallas or Houston on a whim, but to us, going to Dallas was like going to the moon."

"Nobody had any money back then, but the Box family was worse off than most of us. They had a harder time of it." [4]

2

Getting Cotton from Rocks

Train up a child in the way he should go, and when he is old he will not depart from it.

—Proverbs 22:6

Central Texas was a far different place before the coming of the railroad. Stock raising was the primary occupation in this remote part of the world. There was a small amount of subsistence agriculture, but no commercial farming. There was no convenient way to get produce to market.

Then the railroad came to Gatesville in 1882, and the agricultural landscape of Central Texas was transformed overnight. Every hill and valley became a cotton field, and every sizeable town had a cotton gin. Western Coryell County may not look like cotton country, but for a time it was. And the cotton culture was a powerful force that influenced the lives of everyone who grew up there in one way or another.

After the railroad opened the market, cotton became the main cash crop for most families in Jonesboro, and selling cotton was about the only way people generated money to pay their expenses. Farmers also raised wheat and corn, but in the 1920s and '30s, cotton was the money crop.

In some ways, cotton was the perfect crop for this part of the world. There was a system for selling, ginning, and transporting cotton in place. And cotton required no special machinery for harvesting—only two hands and a cotton sack.

But cotton was a mixed blessing. The railroad brought a southern cotton farming culture to a land not always suited for it. Here in the edge of West Texas, the country is prone to fierce storms and lengthy drought. Much of the land is rocky, hilly, of poor quality, and unsuited to the plow, although the Leon River bottomland is rich and productive. Those farmers fortunate enough to farm bottomland were better off than most, while the people who broke submarginal ground, like the Box family, had a much tougher time of it. It is not easy to get cotton and corn from rocks.

And there were great problems with an economy that relied so heavily on a single commodity. Dry land farming, especially here in the edge of West Texas, was risky business. Sometimes the gamble paid off, and sometimes it didn't. When the rain was adequate and timely, crops grew tall and bills got paid, but too often severe droughts, hail storms, blizzards, and even floods wiped out part or all of a farmer's income for an entire year.

Farmers were gamblers by nature. It was in their blood.

In those days, there was no crop insurance or risk management programs. Farmers absorbed losses as best they could. They lived a drought away from financial disaster.

Cloyce Box, like many young men who came of age during the Depression, grew up to be a risk-taker. He learned to gamble from his childhood on the farm.

Of course, the unpredictable weather was only part of the problem for Jonesboro farmers. Market forces almost always worked against the seller and in favor of the buyer. The growing season for cotton did not vary and insured that everyone's harvests always hit the market at the same time—September and October—depressing local prices. Even when good weather and adequate rainfall produced a bumper crop, the greater supply sometimes meant less money in the pocket.

Even though the deck was stacked in favor of the buyer, the amount of acreage planted in cotton dwarfed all other crops. Cotton became so important in this part of Texas that the lives of the people and the affairs of the community revolved around it.

Cotton farming was labor intensive, so most families were large to provide hands for the field. It was not unusual for farm families to have ten children or more.

People paid their bills, bought new shoes, voted, and paid their taxes after the cotton crop came in. Summer vacation in the modern school calendar is nothing more than a modification for what was once an agricultural society. In the summertime, the family needed all hands on deck to work the fields. Children returned to school in the fall, but only after the cotton was picked and ginned.

A specialized economic system emerged with the growing dependency on cotton. It was called *credit*. People lived on credit all year until the cotton crop was picked, ginned, and sold in the fall. In a good year, the money from cotton covered the bill that had been accumulating for the past twelve months at the store with a little left over to order new shoes for the kids from the Sears and Roebuck catalog.

But cotton money sometimes fell short of expenses, trapping farmers in debt. When credit was stretched to the limit, families stayed alive eating green beans, collard greens, corn on the cob, potatoes, and any wild animal they could shoot including squirrels, rabbits, possums, raccoons, and armadillos. A carefully carved piece of cardboard covered the holes in old shoes.

The kind of credit-based economy practiced in the rural parts of Central Texas produced a cycle of debt that was difficult to escape. Some farmers worked sunup to sundown six days a week and never got ahead. It was a dirty, miserable existence—working all the time and going further in the hole. When a farmer maxed out his credit, it was not uncommon for the family to pack up its meager belongings, siphon a few gallons of gasoline, and slip away in the middle of the night, leaving nothing behind but a pile of garbage and a stack of unpaid bills.

Even if a man desired to move his family to Temple, Waco, Fort Worth, or Dallas to take a factory job with a fixed wage and company benefits, the mortgage and the farm debt he incurred kept him returning to the cotton fields, year after year, trapped in a never-ending cycle of poverty and hopelessness.

So, the economic well-being of the people in Jonesboro rose and fell with the fickle price of cotton, and for much of the 1920s and '30s, the price was moving in the wrong direction—pushed one way and then the other by events on the other side of the world.

Agricultural commodity prices in Texas spiked right after World War I, but then began a dramatic free fall when the European farm industry returned to full production after the war. Europe stopped importing American cotton and grain, causing a slow and steady decline in the economies of Coryell and Hamilton counties.

The drop in prices was hard on everyone, but catastrophic for small-scale farmers. When prices dropped, farmers planted more to make up for lost income, but that only made matters worse. Overproduction, combined with a declining market, caused prices to free fall even more.

In June 1920, the price of corn was $1.85 a bushel. By December 1921, the price had dropped to 41 cents. Over that same period, wheat dropped from $2.58 a bushel to 92 cents. But the worst for people around Jonesboro was when the price of cotton tumbled from a high of 42 cents a pound in 1920 to 10 cents in 1921. The price of hogs (poor man's livestock) fell 50 percent.

Farm prices generally rebounded between 1921 and 1925, but sank lower in the last half of the decade. Then the stock market crashed in 1929, and agricultural prices completely collapsed. Some farm produce couldn't be given away and was left rotting in the fields—not worth the trouble to harvest. Thousands of cotton bales purchased the previous year had no buyers and still sat on the docks at the port of Houston. When the next crop arrived, the wharves were still stacked to the rafters with cotton no one wanted.

The glut caused prices to fall off the charts. Cotton prices that had rebounded to 18 cents a pound at the beginning of 1931 dropped to 5 cents by the end of the year—lower than in 1921. Even at fire sale prices, little cotton moved from the warehouses and docks. The demand for cotton had hit rock bottom because people throughout the world had stopped buying new clothes. No one wanted cotton at any price.[1]

There was no industry to speak of in Coryell County, so the citizens of Jonesboro were hogtied to agriculture whether they liked it or not. When the bottom dropped out of the cotton market, many families reverted to subsistence farming and hunting, just like in the nineteenth century. Some farmers augmented their meager incomes by cutting cedar posts, but chopping cedar with an ax was a hard way to make a dollar, especially at a few pennies a post. Other hillside farmers hired out to chop a neighbor's bottomland cotton for a dollar a day. (Cotton had to be thinned out after it sprouted to maximize yield.) Those things aside, and except for bootlegging and stealing (and there was plenty of that going on), there was nothing farmers could do but plow their fields, plant their crops, and quietly accept the price determined in some faraway place by mysterious economic forces they could not understand.

Farmers who owned their land outright could scratch by, but the ones with mortgages were caught between a rock and a hard place. Some farmers lost their farms because they couldn't make enough to pay their taxes. Others couldn't make their mortgage payments. The number of farm foreclosures rose dramatically in the 1930s.

Poverty spread like gossip at the beauty parlor. People were malnourished. Children went to bed hungry. The Great Depression came early to Coryell and Hamilton counties and it hit like a Joe Louis right hand.

There was precious little money in circulation. The wealth of the people was in the dirt they plowed and crops they raised. Bartering for goods and services was a common practice. Houses had no electricity, running water, telephone, air-conditioning, or flush toilets. Those kinds of modern conveniences were fast becoming necessities in urban areas all across America, but were science fiction to people in Jonesboro. Large American cities were electrified before the turn of the century, while rural Texans languished in flickering candlelight for two more generations.

No one had a savings account, IRA, health insurance, or retirement plan. Most folks planned to drag a cotton sack until the day they dropped dead in the field. A vacation was something from a romance novel. A college education was a pipe dream and a useless waste of time, not to mention financially unattainable. Only rich city kids went to college.

A surprising number of people around Jonesboro came into this world, lived their entire lives, and went out again without seeing a doctor or a dentist. Some of them never saw a movie, heard recorded music, or owned a toothbrush.

Still, the people did the best they could with what they had. A few farm families owned tractors, but most farmers, like the Boxes, plowed one row at a time with mules, just like in the nineteenth century. With a team of mules and a walking plow, a farmer could work 2 acres on a good day. (A modern-day farmer with a diesel tractor and a sixteen-row cultivator can till an acre in 10 minutes.) That kind of farming was backbreaking work, especially in the triple-digit heat of a long Texas summer. By the time a farmer reached the age of 45, he was past his prime—physically worn out and used up.

He was spiritually and emotionally drained as well. In the 1930s, there was a depression of the soul as well as the pocketbook. Too many people found life bleak, hopeless, and without joy. There was an absence of humor and excitement. Each day was a physical challenge followed by the night that was long, dark, and silent.

Financial uncertainty and a high level of stress placed rural people at greater risk of disease (both physical and psychological) and death. People snapped under the pressure. Families fell apart. Murder and suicide rates climbed during the 1930s.

For many children, the day-to-day stress of living in poverty became a powerful force in their adult lives. Poverty caused some young people to lose all hope, while others grew desperate to escape their misery whatever the cost.

The head of the household was particularly vulnerable to stress. Men, taught since childhood to be tough in all situations and to keep their feelings locked inside, had no safe release for their anger and disappointment. Some of them crawled inside a whiskey bottle or ended it all with a bullet to the brain. Others took their frustrations out on their wives and children. Some just ran away.

The Box family knew firsthand the effects of poverty on the man of the house. R. D. Box Jr., raised in the western tradition to be the breadwinner, had his pride and dignity slowly stripped away by financial hardship. The constant pressure of providing for his family slowly broke his spirit. He turned dark and moody. And there was tension between R. D. and Zelma, exacerbated by financial problems and his unhealthy mental state.

Then in 1936 the family fell apart. First, R. D. Sr. died, and when he did, his son slipped deeper into depression. Soon after that, Robert D. Box Jr. reached the breaking point. One night as his family slept, R. D. slipped away and left Zelma to raise their four children alone. The twins were thirteen years old. Just when they needed their father the most, he was gone.

"It was an awful time for Boyce and Cloyce," L. Louise Box (Boyce's wife) said. "They just woke up one morning, and their dad was gone. They learned later that Mr. Box had a nervous breakdown. His family didn't know where he was for at least a year. Actually he was in Waco at the VA Hospital."[2]

With no man around, there was little money coming in and little food in the pantry. Cloyce and Boyce tried to take up the slack. Cloyce, more than the other children, assumed the leadership role in the family, but there was only so much he could do. Mrs. Box refused to let her children drop out of school. Instead, she worked day and night to keep food on the table. She sold the better of the two farms to pay taxes and other bills, and the family moved to "the mountain place."

The house on the mountain was old and run down. When it rained, the roof leaked like a milk strainer, and the wind blew straight through cracks in the walls with barely a pause. The thin porous walls with no insulation and gaps big enough to see daylight on the other side let in summer breezes, but made the house almost impossible to heat in the wintertime. One cold winter morning, Cloyce and Boyce woke to find that snow had drifted through the cracks and dusted their bed during the night.

Zelma nailed tin can lids over holes in the floor to keep out rattlesnakes that crawled under the house. Once a year, the Box twins would hitchhike into Gatesville and search the back alleys and garbage dumps for cardboard and old license plates. They tacked the cardboard to the inside walls of their house to block the winter wind and nailed the old license plates over holes in the roof to slow down the rain that trickled into the living room.[3]

"My father's family barely got by," Cloyce's son Tom explained. "They lived in a house with thin walls, no electricity, and no running water. There was little food in the house. They wore hand-me-down clothes the neighbors left on the doorstep. My father and Uncle Boyce would hunt rabbits with a .22 rifle. They had to shoot something if they wanted to eat. Dad's lifelong love of hunting came from those early days shooting rabbits in Jonesboro."[4]

Even in desperate times there were lighter moments. On summer afternoons, the twins swam naked in the Leon River. Cloyce liked to put girls in the cellar and stand on the door until they screamed.[5]

But on the whole there was not much to smile about.

"It was a hurtful time for the children," L. Louise Box recalled. "Boyce and Cloyce never had much to say about it. I suppose the memories of that time were too painful, so they kept quiet. There was no money and just the barest of necessities. Even poor people called them poor. And not everyone was nice to them. When they hitchhiked to Gatesville, some of their neighbors just drove on by like they weren't there. That hurt Boyce and Cloyce."

"But most people were good to them. There was a lady named Mrs. Sellers who was always kind. She gave them food and clothes. One year at Christmas someone left a basket of fruit on their front porch. That was the best Christmas they had."[6]

Many people in the community rallied around the family. "Orzo and Mae Sims were the most wonderful people," wrote sister Wilmuth. "They fed us often on the way from school."[7]

"But Mrs. Box kept the family from falling apart," L. Louise Box continued. "She had a strong personality. She was such a proud woman. She had been to college (Tyler Junior College) when she was young, and she took a lot of pride in that. She met Mr. Box when she came home to take care of her ailing father. She was a devout woman—a died-in-the-wool Church of Christ. There was no whiskey in her house and no bad language. She never learned to drive a car (someone drove her to church every Sunday), and she never watched her sons play basketball, but she did everything she could for them."

"She was devastated when her husband left, and to an extent she was ostracized by the community. Back then a woman was expected to stick with her man no matter what. Divorce was a rare thing, and it stigmatized the woman, especially in the Church of Christ. A lot of people looked down on her when her husband left."[8]

Wilmuth Box Johnson recalled that her mother "was ashamed by R. D.'s leaving. That's pretty much of an insult and very rare. Dad was the only man I knew that had left his family."[9]

But pride was Zelma's shield against social rejection. L. Louise Box remembered that "Mrs. Box always kept her head up, even when people whispered behind her back."[10]

Wilmuth noted that her mother "took great pride in everything. Her appearance especially. Always neat and clean. Never saw her in an un-starched or unironed dress."

Cloyce too was a man with eye for detail and a fondness for spit and polish—one of the many traits he inherited from his mother.

And Zelma ran her household with a firm hand. "We never questioned mother," Wilmuth said. "Whatever she said, we did. After all she was keeping us all going."[11]

But as bad as things were for the Box family, things were about to get worse. The Box kids were still reeling from their dad's sudden departure for parts unknown when Mrs. Box, the cornerstone and provider for the family, took to her bed with fever, chills, and persistent coughing. The doctor came up from Gatesville, diagnosed her illness as tuberculosis, and blamed the disease on the damp, drafty house. The county health authorities, fearing an epidemic, sent Zelma to one of the state tuberculosis institutions for quarantine.

Most families would have disintegrated under the pressure of a broken home, but the Box children were lucky to live in a village like Jonesboro where people looked after each other.

Cloyce, Boyce, Wilmuth, and Janice walked several miles each day to the school in Jonesboro. The school was their sanctuary and their place of stability when their family fell apart. At school, the Box children quickly came to know and love the Jonesboro superintendent—a remarkable man named Purlie Thomas Lemmons. Mr. Lemmons became their lifelong mentor and friend. When Mrs. Box was in the sanitarium fighting tuberculosis, Mr. Lemmons saw to it that the Box kids were taken care of.

"My father and his brother and sisters lived for a time with Mr. Lemmons," Tom Box recalled. "Mr. and Mrs. Lemmons just took them in. No questions asked. Later they lived with a young couple in a little community nearby. The young man and his wife were in their twenties. They were barely making it as it was. But they took my dad and his siblings in and treated them like family."[12]

At different times, the Box children lived with Blake and Alice Lovelace and with the Kitchens family at Levita. Still, Cloyce, Boyce, Wilmuth, and Janice could have become wards of the state had it not been for Mr. Lemmons.

"A special bond developed between Cloyce Box and P. T. Lemmons," Cloyce's friend Maurice Campbell said. "Mr. Lemmons was like a father to both the Box boys. He encouraged them and took care of them. He bought Cloyce and Boyce shoes so they could play basketball."[13]

"Boyce always said that in a way it was a good thing his father left," L. Louise Box explained, "because if he had stayed, Boyce and Cloyce would have never left that old rocky farm. Their dad would have wanted them to stay, and they would have. They would never have gone against their father. That's the way they were raised."

"But when Mr. Box left, that created an opportunity for Mr. Lemmons to come into their lives. He saw potential in them, and gave them a vision of a world beyond the place they lived. He gave them dreams."[14]

P. T. Lemmons was born in Pocahontas, Arkansas, in the northeastern part of the state where the Mississippi Delta gives way to the Ozarks. His family moved to Tolar, Texas when Mr. Lemmons was three years old. His father, A. M. Lemmons, was a cotton farmer and a Church of Christ preacher.

He hated the name Purlie and insisted that everyone call him P. T., although as an adult he garnered so much respect that everyone, even men and women many years his senior, could only call him Mr. Lemmons.

P. T. Lemmons earned a bachelor's degree from Abilene Christian College and his masters at Baylor University in Waco. He was a teacher and coach at Stephens Hill in Erath County and at Ewing in Coryell County (now a part of the Fort Hood military reservation). In 1927 Jonesboro hired Mr. Lemmons as a combination teacher, coach, principal, and superintendent, although his reputation as a basketball coach probably clinched the deal.

Jonesboro got the bargain of a lifetime. Mr. Lemmons ran the school in Jonesboro from 1927 to 1972. Charles Lindbergh flew solo from New York to Paris in Mr. Lemmons' first year at Jonesboro, and he retired three years after Neil Armstrong walked on the moon. He worked year to year, never taking a multi-year contract.

No one dared question his honesty, his integrity, or his authority. There was no need to.

His influence on that small Texas town is immeasurable. He was there so long, he became the moral and spiritual embodiment of the community. His students revered him. They sought his advice and his blessing. No one wanted to embarrass him or disappoint him.

He kept the school alive during the Great Depression, World War II, and the 1960s when many small communities lost their schools to consolidation. He was the living example of rural conservative values from the Bible Belt. In the turbulent '60s, while America went to hell in a hand basket, Mr. Lemmons stood as a bastion against the drug culture, Vietnam War protestors, and hippies in California.

He was generous to a fault. The four Box children were recipients of what people around Jonesboro still call the first free school lunch program in Texas—quietly paid for by Mr. Lemmons out of his own pocket.

And his treatment of the Box kids was just a part of the job for Mr. Lemmons. No child went hungry or did without school supplies on his watch. For forty-five years he took care of four generations of Robucks, Lilljedahls, Mayhews, Massingills, Sellers, Dyers, Youngs, and Watsons.

Mr. Lemmons lived for basketball—a game he first played on a dirt court at Tolar. He used the sport as a way to touch the lives of his students and win their respect.

In forty years, his Jonesboro Eagles played 947 games—winning 729 (76.9%). Year after year, the Eagles were a perennial Class B power. In the 1950s and '60s Jonesboro advanced to the Class B regional basketball playoffs 16 of 17 years.

Mr. Lemmons died on April 5, 1995 at Forest Oaks Nursing Home in Hamilton, Texas. He was ninety-four years old. The Jonesboro gymnasium was the only appropriate place for the funeral and the only building big enough to hold the crowd.

If there were Catholics in Jonesboro, P. T. Lemmons would be a saint.

3

The Giraffes of West Texas

Ability is a poor man's wealth.

—John Wooden

P. T. Lemmons had a keen eye for athletic talent, and he knew he had made a rare discovery the first time he saw "Big Box" (Boyce) and "Little Box" (Cloyce) playing basketball in their bare feet on the dirt court at Jonesboro School. In those days, children dreamed of playing Jonesboro Eagle basketball at a young age (there was no football team), and in that way the Box twins were no different from the other boys. But on another level, Cloyce and Boyce Box were unlike any young athletes P. T. Lemmons had ever seen.

The game came easily and naturally to them. Cloyce and Boyce were bigger, faster, stronger, and more aggressive than the other boys their age, and even though they were new to the game, they could easily out dribble, out jump, and out play even the older guys. As the twins matured in their teens, they grew taller, stronger, and faster, and they mastered every sport they tried without much effort. Cloyce could hit a baseball into the next county and run like a scalded dog. Boyce was a natural at the plate, and his pitching arm, as the old saying goes, could "throw sunrise past a rooster."

In any contest of running, jumping, and throwing, the Box twins were light-years ahead of the competition. They dominated track meets, often scoring enough points between them to win the event.

Their coach had seen some good athletes in his day, but nothing to compare to Cloyce and Boyce Box. A coach was lucky if athletes with their talent came along once in a lifetime. The Box twins were special, and P. T. Lemmons quickly took them under his wing.

Mr. Lemmons taught the Box twins to play basketball, but he also taught them to be winners. When it came to sports, the coach was in it to win, and he made no apologies for it. "I have one philosophy in athletics and that's to win," Mr. Lemmons once said. "Win fairly, but win."[1] The Box twins revered their coach and bought in to his philosophy.

The Jonesboro Eagles soared when Big Box and Little Box were on the court. The twins could dribble, pass, play defense, block shots, and score at will. It was not unusual for Cloyce and Boyce to score all the points for their team. They weren't ball hogs; they were just so much better than everyone else was.

There was an unusual chemistry between them that allowed them to communicate without speaking. Cloyce would sometimes release the pass before Boyce broke for the basket.

With their height, speed, and quickness, they overpowered and systematically dismantled the far less gifted opponents at Turnersville, Oglesby, Flat, Cranfill's Gap, and Walnut Springs. Their fame grew with every game they played.

Many children raised in poverty are beaten down by daily survival and lose the ability to dream, but an extraordinary talent at basketball taught the Box twins that nothing was beyond their reach. As they racked up points, victories, and championships, they gained poise and self-confidence. Basketball empowered them and made them feel important.

The world treated them special because they could play basketball. Other children who once made fun of them now admired them. Adults flattered them. Cloyce and Boyce sensed the admiration and the flattery, and the sensation gave them a feeling of superiority. Basketball lifted them above their impoverished conditions, and gave them something to hold on to for the rest of their lives.

Many contemporaries considered Boyce the better athlete, but there was a mental toughness about Cloyce that was not as pronounced in his twin. Boyce was a kind boy—gentle and tenderhearted, but Cloyce had a more aggressive nature and a fiery competitive spirit that concealed whatever compassion was inside. Even then people knew there was something extraordinary about him. Nothing would stand between Cloyce Box and the things he wanted.

Of the two, Cloyce was more like his mother. Zelma was a stern woman with a fierce pride in her family. She lived in grinding poverty, but she never accepted it or gave in to it. She had been to college, and she regretted dropping out for the rest of her life.

Despite her difficulties, there was a streak of quiet arrogance about her, and she passed that quality on to Cloyce. She saw greatness in him before anyone else. She knew Cloyce had special gifts, and she pampered him to the point of vanity. Cloyce became the focus of her hopes and dreams, and he spent the rest of her life trying to please her. Cloyce could do no wrong in her eyes, and as a consequence he developed a precocious sense of his own abilities.

"You will do great things," Zelma told both of her sons, and they believed her.

"You can go places," Mr. Lemmons told them, and that's what they did.

Groomed in that environment, Cloyce Box grew up, not just with his self-respect and ambitions intact, but with a formidable self-confidence and drive. He was born with an engaging and forceful personality. He made a powerful first impression, and most people took an instant liking to him. He was a rational, temperate man, yet wildly ambitious. He longed to be somebody, and he believed he was destined to accomplish something important.

He was a natural leader, and even as a young man, other people deferred to him and pushed him to the front. He could be physically intimidating, and his ability to dominate those around him began with his size. When fully grown, he stood 6'4" and looked down on everybody. He was a twentieth-century Apollo—tall, handsome, athletic, charismatic, and intelligent.

But basketball was his ticket out of poverty. Jonesboro, Texas, was not a place where dreams come true, especially for a talented and ambitious young man whose hands didn't fit a plow handle. So, with Mr. Lemmons' help and Zelma Box's approval, Cloyce Box got out of Jonesboro by playing basketball, although no one who knew him at the time could have guessed just how far and how high he would go.

"Basketball coaches all over the state respected P. T. Lemmons," Maurice Campbell explained. "Mr. Lemmons had some connections with the athletic department at West Texas State Teachers College in Canyon, Texas (now West Texas A&M). He helped Cloyce and Boyce get a scholarship."[2]

That connection was Gus Miller. Coach Miller, former basketball coach at Texas Wesleyan College in Fort Worth, had been to Jonesboro before. In 1938, Miller recruited Cullen Walsh from a Jonesboro cotton field. Walsh, a 6'3" redhead, became a star basketball player at Texas Wesleyan.

Miller knew a good basketball program when he saw one, and he put P. T. Lemmons on the top of his contact list after watching the Box twins run rings around the opposition in a high school tournament in Fort Worth.

When Gus Miller left Texas Wesleyan for West Texas State in 1941, he never forgot the Jonesboro juggernauts. In the spring of 1942, with high school graduation looming, Coach Miller drove his old Ford sedan to the mountain place and convinced Zelma Box to let her sons play basketball in Canyon.[3]

Zelma Box sent her sons to college with her blessing although their absence from the farm would be an unspeakable hardship for her. In her heart, she knew that Cloyce and Boyce could do great things if given an opportunity. This was their chance, maybe their only chance, to get out, so she gave them a hug and a kiss and gently shoved them out the door.

Boyce graduated from Jonesboro High School in May 1941, but Cloyce graduated a year later after dropping out for a time to work and support his brother and sisters while his mother was sick. Boyce spent the year after his graduation working in California. Then in the summer of 1942, Cloyce and Boyce packed everything they owned in a small bag and hitchhiked 400 miles from Jonesboro to their new home on the high plains.

L. Louise Box told of their adventures on the road. "When they left Jonesboro that summer, they had two dollars between them—payment for chopping cotton. They were just a couple of wide-eyed country boys, ready to take on the world. It took several days of hitchhiking for them to get from Jonesboro to Canyon. I guess they slept on the side of the road if they slept at all."

"Then a man picked them up in Plainview (Hail County), I think it was. He took them to Canyon and let them out on the square. It was around midnight. There was a hotel on the square. It's still there. The man told them that since the hour was late, they could probably get a good rate on a room. So they rented a room for a dollar."

"The next day they spent their last dollar for some food. Then they walked over to the campus and checked into their dorm that afternoon. Neither of them had a cent in their pockets."

"Their first job at West Texas State was in the cafeteria," L. Louise continued. "The ladies in the cafeteria looked after them. They also worked on farms around Canyon on weekends and in the summer. And with their scholarship they got $25 laundry money. They thought they were rich. They even sent money to their mother in Jonesboro."[4]

There is a family story connected with their first day at West Texas State. The story goes that when Cloyce and Boyce first met with the basketball coaches, they were embarrassed about being from a tiny town no one had heard of, so they told the coaches they were from Waco.

"Is that near Jonesboro?" one of the coaches asked. "I hear there are two guys there who are pretty good."[5]

Wilmuth recalled the times that Cloyce would "hitch hike home to see mom and me. Then after the visit, I'd take him out to the Highway 36 turnaround and drive off. [That was] the hardest thing I ever did. Mom never went with me. She stayed home and had her cry while I was gone. I never saw my mother cry that I can remember. She was so tough. Our lives were very hard but Cloyce sent an allotment for us to live on. We were better off than we ever dreamed to be."[6]

The Box twins were homesick at first, but they quickly adjusted to life in a college town. The accommodations alone sold them on the place. The Buffalo Courts athletic dormitory (today the Alumni Center) was the most luxurious living quarters they had ever seen and a far cry from their shack in the cedar brakes. The two-story dorm was built of 143 tons of petrified wood hauled from a New

Mexico riverbed and constructed during the Depression by athletes with help from the Works Progress Administration. It opened in 1935 as the state's first dormitory for athletes. It had running water, electric lights, indoor flush toilets, and seven-and-one-half-foot beds to accommodate tall basketball players.

But the biggest surprise for the Box twins was the quality of the basketball program at West Texas State, for unbeknownst to them, Cloyce and Boyce had arrived at the Mecca of 1940s small college basketball. The West Texas State Buffaloes were not your average basketball team. Here on the Texas plains was a program with world-class talent, a crafty and eccentric coach, and a national reputation as a basketball powerhouse.

Cloyce and Boyce Box knew little about West Texas State before they arrived in Canyon, but the rest of the world was well acquainted with the lofty Buffaloes. Sports writers from New York to California described West Texas State as the tallest basketball team in the world. One writer quipped, "Buffaloes, hell, they're giraffes." *Time Magazine* agreed, calling Coach Al Baggett's team the "Giraffes of West Texas."[7]

But they played like hungry cheetahs. First time opponents expected the big guys from Canyon to play a slow, deliberate game and were surprised to discover the Buffaloes played a flashy run-and-gun brand of basketball, similar to big fancy colleges in the East and the Midwest, whom they often trounced.

The man who built the program, Al Baggett, was a big, loud, and energetic fellow with a larger-than-life personality. When he came to Canyon from Amarillo College in 1933, few people cared about the Buffalo basketball program. Football was king in these parts. Basketball was something a few dozen bored spectators came in out of the cold to watch during the winter months.

Baggett changed that in a hurry. He established a relationship and a network with high school coaches all over Texas and the southwest, and through that network, he gathered information about the best basketball talent. He then used his colorful personality and considerable recruiting skills to attract the best and tallest basketball players he could find.

The 1936 team averaged 6'6". The national press labeled that squad the tallest basketball team on earth, and after that the tall guys just kept coming. Soon the tall Texans from Canyon were the talk of the basketball world.

The team was an extension of their coach's loud and brassy personality. Once on a trip to New York, a young Al Baggett saw the Harlem Globetrotters at Madison Square Garden. He loved the athleticism and the theatrics of the Globetrotters, so he created a version of that great barnstorming team on the high plains of West Texas. He even designed gaudy uniforms with knee socks featuring long vertical stripes that made the players look even taller and kneepads with big stars on the front. Win or lose, the team put on a show.

But the Buffaloes were more than color and style. They could play, and by the time Cloyce and Boyce Box arrived in Canyon in the summer of 1942, West Texas State had built a national reputation for basketball excellence. The Buffaloes were 26-4 in 1938–39 and 26-8 in 1939–40. The 1940–41 varsity squad reached the final four of the NAIA (National Association of Intercollegiate Athletics) tournament for the first time in the school's history.

The 1941–42 team was the best yet; finishing the season 28-2. That year, the Buffaloes won the Oklahoma City Invitational Tournament, and breezed through the Border Conference schedule without a loss. Articles about the team appeared in *Time*, *Look*, *Life*, *Colliers*, and *Esquire* magazines. For a time that spring, West Texas State ranked number one in the nation, quite a feat for a tiny school in the middle of nowhere.

The Buffaloes had a simple strategy. They played basketball with a hair trigger. When they had the ball at their own end of the court, they loaded up and took a wang at it.

"There's nothing mysterious about it," Coach Baggett once said. "The object of basketball is to put the ball into the pocket as often as possible, and that's what we try to do."

"If we don't shoot 90 times a game," he added, "we feel the evening is wasted."[8]

The Buffaloes played to the crowd, with a relentless assault on the basket from beginning to end and not much defense. While putting up 90 to 100 shots a game, even shooting at around 30%, the Buffaloes scored between 60 and 70 points, and on those nights when they were hot, they could light up the scoreboard like the Fourth of July and humiliate the other team.

Their upbeat style of basketball was fun to play and even more fun to watch—a precursor to the modern game. Fans from New York to Los Angeles packed the gym whenever the Buffaloes were in town. The stars of the team in the early 1940s were 6'10" center Charles "Chick" Halbert; burly, high-scoring All-American forward Price Brookfield; and slick-shooting forward Jack Maddox.[9]

Led by Halbert, Brookfield, and Maddox, the Buffaloes could play with any team in the country. In 1942, West Texas State scored one hundred points three times, an almost unheard of event in those days. In twenty-six games in 1942, the skyscrapers from Canyon played to well over 100,000 fans, including 40,000 in three games at the National Invitational Tournament at Madison Square Garden in New York City. In the most exciting game of the weekend, 18,117 spectators packed the Garden to watch the Buffaloes play the Long Island University (LIU) Blackbirds. Thousands more waiting outside in a snowstorm had to be turned away.

Even though LIU beat West Texas State in overtime, New Yorkers were captivated by the Buffaloes from West Texas. East coast Writer Bob Considine spoke for many New Yorkers when he wrote, "Texas lost, presumably to the better club. But we'd go to see those elongated south westerners every night of the week. Their incredible size alone is a lure."[10]

In the spring of 1942, West Texas State basketball was one of the few subjects not completely overshadowed by the Japanese attack on Pearl Harbor and the American entry into the war. In fact, the Buffaloes reached the pinnacle of their success at the Oklahoma City Tournament when they won four straight games including convincing victories over Oklahoma A&M and the Arkansas Razorbacks, champions of the Southwest Conference. That year, the basketball program made more money than the football program—a most unusual turn of events for a small school in football-crazy West Texas.[11] The buzz around the country was that the incoming freshmen class, including a set of twin towers from somewhere near Waco, was the best ever.

As Al Baggett told a reporter, "You ain't seen nothin' yet."

The West Texas State basketball team was so formidable in those years that some opponents took extraordinary measures just to stay in the game with the tree top Texans from Canyon. Coach Baggett told the story of an unusual tactic employed by St. Mary's in a game in San Antonio. Whenever the Rattlers tried to shoot from close range, the tall Buffaloes blocked the shots, so St. Mary's moved to the perimeter and began dropping bombs from way outside.

What was unusual, and suspicious, was that St. Mary's got more than its share of the offensive rebounds. The missed shots took enormous bounces off the hoop and backboard. Often times the lively ball bounced all the way to midcourt.

Coach Baggett smelled a rat and called time out to look at the ball. By his own account he dropped the ball to floor, and it bounced almost to the ceiling. It seems that Mose Simms, the crafty St. Mary's coach, had pumped fifteen pounds of air into the game ball that was only supposed to hold seven.[12]

4

Uncle Sam's Team

Life is change. Growth is optional. Choose wisely.

—Anonymous

The war was the only thing that could turn the Buffalo basketball stampede, and by the spring of 1942, the war news was not good. Victory would not be a slam dunk.

In January, the Japanese began the siege of Bataan. By summer, the Imperial Army controlled Singapore, Hong Kong, Wake Island, and the Philippines. In Europe, the Battle of Britain was raging. The Nazis had been in Paris for a year.

For Americans at home, gas rationing kicked in, limiting each household to three gallons a week. Congress passed the first peacetime draft legislation in 1940, and then in 1942 lowered the draft age from 21 to 18. There were 1.8 million men in uniform (army, navy, marines) in 1941. By the summer of 1942, that number had swelled to 3.9 million.

The new draft law hit college campuses and their athletic teams especially hard. An able-bodied young man in civvies was a rare sight on the streets of Canyon and Amarillo. The future of Buffalo basketball was about to be sacrificed for a higher cause.

The coach was among the first to go. In the summer of 1942, Al Baggett was commissioned an army captain and assigned to the Third Air Corps District in Tulsa, Oklahoma, as the Director of Physical Training. Later he served in North Africa and in Europe.

To replace Baggett, West Texas State promoted William Augustus "Gus" Miller to head basketball coach. Miller had been hired as an assistant coach a few months earlier.

Coach Miller came with outstanding credentials. He had an impressive record at Texas Wesleyan, winning 101 of 113 basketball games in four seasons, including a victory over the West Texas State Buffaloes, the "World's Tallest Basketball Team," on December 27, 1938, in the Oklahoma City Tournament. Coach Miller was a West Texas State alumnus who had coached basketball and football at high schools in Slaton, Texas, and Trinidad, Colorado, before taking the basketball job at Texas Wesleyan.

Miller had big sneakers to fill, but he was born with big feet. With Gus Miller in charge, the 1942–43 Buffalo varsity basketball team had a record of 15-7 and was cochampions of the Border Conference. The cochampionship was the result of an upset by Arizona in the finals of the conference tournament—the Buffaloes only conference loss.

Even with wartime travel restrictions in place and a shortened schedule, the Buffaloes played to large crowds in Philadelphia, Pennsylvania, and Buffalo, New York. The team competed in the Metropolitan Basketball Tournament in Madison Square Garden and in the All College Basketball Tournament in Oklahoma City.

The 1942–43 Buffalo freshmen team seemed destined to be the best ever and a sure bet to extend the Buffalo basketball legacy. The team was talented and tall. Cloyce Box, Boyce Box, and Metz Lafollette from McKinney, Texas, stood 6'4".[1] Glenn Braden from Dorchester, Texas, was 6'5". Ray Ellefson from Minneapolis, Minnesota, was 6'9". The runt, Eugene Keating of Fort Worth, was only 6'2".[2]

Before 1942, there was a rule in the Border Conference prohibiting freshmen from playing varsity sports. Then all colleges suffered from a wartime shortage of male athletes prompting the Border Conference to suspend the rule prohibiting freshmen from playing on the varsity. The suspension of the rules allowed Cloyce and Boyce Box and the rest of the 1942–43 Buffalo freshmen to travel and play with the varsity, but they also played a separate freshman schedule.

And they were good. Some experts rated them the finest collection of freshmen basketball talent in the country. The Buffalo freshmen were unbeaten against other freshman squads, scoring 650 points (averaging over 70 points a game) while allowing only

308 (an average of 34 points a game). The smallest winning margin was seventeen points.

That year, the Buffalo freshmen won the tournament in Dumas, Texas, winning three games in an afternoon. Boyce Box scored 142 points that year and was the high scoring freshman. Cloyce was just behind scoring 136 points.

Coach Miller called his freshmen "the greatest aggregation of first year men" he had ever coached.[3] During the season, Miller often used the freshmen as shock troops, as he did when the varsity fell behind Arizona State in the 1943 Border Conference Tournament. The freshmen went on a scoring spree and pulled the game out of the fire.

In normal times, a talented group of underclassmen would have caused an epidemic of basketball fever among panhandle sports fans, but these were not normal times. The young athletes who played basketball at West Texas State were also prime draft age, and by the spring of 1943, many of them had joined the military. The war put the giraffes of West Texas out of business. The shoes worn by the "Tallest Team on Earth" were stacked in Burton Gym with no feet to fill them. Gus Miller was not encouraged.

"Our plans for the future will depend on the progress of the war," he said. "We do not have a single man on the campus who either played with our varsity or freshmen teams last season."

"They're all gone," the coach added, "but we do have the tradition that will go a long way in getting us on the beam in basketball after the war."[4]

Years later, basketball fans wondered just how good that team would have been had its progress not been interrupted by World War II.

The loss of athletes to military service, combined with an overall decline in enrollment, prompted the Committee on Athletics to drop all intercollegiate sports at West Texas State for the duration of the war, although the committee would later reverse itself and allow a limited schedule in some sports. Still, the initial suspension of athletics prompted a fear that the best athletes, the talented freshmen basketball squad in particular, might defect to the Southwest Conference when the war ended.

There were regulations in place to keep athletes from jumping schools and schools from raiding each other's rosters. But that technicality didn't prevent the Southwest Conference, along with most other major conferences in the country, from passing a new rule that permitted an athlete from another school to finish his eligibility at a Southwest Conference institution when his own school discontinued sports.

Then in December 1942, the Southwest Conference suspended the 1-year transfer rule. (Athletes who transferred from one school to another normally had to sit out a full season.)[5] Out on the plains, it seemed obvious that big schools were gearing up to take advantage of the small schools. In Canyon, the line formed to the left.

But for now, there was a cause more important than basketball. Young men all across America had to put aside their own dreams to save the country.

Sometimes we forget just how young they really were. Many of them were just out of high school, or younger, when the war started, and they went off to war without a clue of what they were getting into. Some had never been on a date. Some didn't shave or drive a car. Some of them joined the military, shipped out to Europe or the Pacific, defeated the enemy, returned home, and still could not vote or legally buy beer.

Cloyce Box, like many young men of his generation, didn't wait for the draft. He joined the US Marines in November 1942 as a part of the V-12 Naval College Training Program—a wartime plan to address the shortage of commissioned officers in the navy and marines. Box's agreement with the US Marines allowed him to remain in school, at least for a time, under a clause entitled "detached for special services." He had to pass a rigorous exam to qualify for the program and maintain at least a C average to stay in it. The program also required that he behave himself, have good morals, and otherwise stay in good graces with the marines.

In addition to his regular college courses, Box took special classes to teach him how to be a marine officer. If he did not keep up his grades or if he acted in ways unbecoming of a marine officer, the Commandant could send him elsewhere or even waive college altogether in favor of active duty. Brother Boyce also signed up for the program as did Glenn Braden, Eugene Keating, and Metz

Lafollette. By 1943, the entire Buffalo freshmen basketball squad had joined Uncle Sam's team.

For Cloyce and Boyce Box, going off to war was a Box family tradition—something rural southern men had always done without a second thought. Cloyce's great-grandfather fought with Sam Houston in the Texas Revolution. In 1862, Cloyce's grandfather, R. D. Box Sr., served in the 17th Texas Cavalry. Cloyce's dad, R. D. Box Jr., served in the US Army, the 132nd Field Artillery Regiment, a part of the 36th Division. The 132nd shipped to France in August 1918, trained under French officers near Paris, and was pronounced ready for service six weeks later, but the armistice was signed before the regiment deployed for combat.

Cloyce stayed in Canyon for the first six months of his assignment. Then in the July 1943, the Marines sent him to Louisiana Polytechnic Institute in Ruston for additional training. The experience would change his life.

Until shipping out to Ruston, Box was a below-average student who struggled with the basic college courses. He flunked freshman English his first semester at West Texas State, took it again in the spring, and withdrew before the end of the semester. Many of his other grades were not much better. He was a fair reader, but his writing was atrocious. Misspelled words and simple grammatical errors filled the letters he wrote home to his mother.

But in Ruston a remarkable transformation occurred. Box learned to believe in his intelligence and his ability as a student. He had a hunger for practical knowledge and a strong desire to make something of himself. At Ruston, he took rigorous courses in algebra, analytical geometry, trigonometry, physics, mechanical drawing, surveying, mechanics, electricity, and magnetism. He struggled, but he passed. In the process, he gained confidence as a student. By December 1944, he had completed most of the coursework for a degree in civil engineering.

He also played basketball for the Bulldogs and played organized football for the first time, although he was not impressed with the game. On September 3, 1944, Louisiana Tech played the Selman Field Cyclones—a team made up of Army Air Force enlistees from Monroe, Louisiana. In the second quarter, Box got loose in the secondary, caught a pass from quarterback Johnny Bibb (from Sweetwater, Texas), and raced 18 yards for his first touchdown.[6]

While Cloyce was in Ruston, Louisiana, the Marines sent Boyce to the University of North Carolina in Chapel Hill. Boyce studied to be a Marine officer and played football and basketball for the Tar Heels (also known as the White Phantoms) in the 1943–44 season. Back in Ruston, Cloyce listened to his brother's football games on the radio.

That winter, the University of North Carolina basketball team won seventeen games, lost ten, and was 9-1 in conference play, losing one of three games to the Duke University Blue Devils. Despite the loss, North Carolina was the 1944 Southern Conference regular season champion and the top seed in the conference tournament in Raleigh, but lost for the second time to Duke in the final round. Boyce Box, the "one-hand sharpshooter from West Texas," finished the year as the Tar Heels second leading scorer, and he made the all-conference team.[7]

In November 1944, the Marines transferred Cloyce to the Marine Corps Recruit Depot in Parris Island, South Carolina, and then to Camp Lejeune in Jacksonville, North Carolina, where he reunited briefly with brother Boyce. Then on April 26, 1945, Cloyce deployed to Tientsin, China, a 2nd Lieutenant in a tank squadron in the 1st Marine Division. He commanded 150 men and 15 tanks.

Cloyce Box served his country well. He was proud to be a marine, and for the rest of his life he carried himself with the bearing of a marine combat officer.

When the war ended, Cloyce and Boyce Box could have taken their basketball skills to any big-time college program in the country (many small college stars did just that), but they were loyal to their teammates and coaches at West Texas State.

"North Carolina offered Boyce a full scholarship after the war," L. Louise Box recalled, "but he turned them down. He missed Canyon, and he missed his brother. They had rarely been apart before going off to war. They couldn't wait to get back to Canyon to see each other and their friends."[8]

They were not alone. During the war, the Canyon campus almost died of neglect, but so many veterans enrolled for classes in the fall of 1946 that the school ran out of housing space. That fall classes did not start until October 1 to give administrators time to deal with the housing crunch, overcrowded classrooms, and record level of enrollment at the college. Even then, the housing shortage led to protests and a student strike, halting classes for several days. The situation cooled when the Veterans Administration threatened to suspend GI Bill payments to strikers.

The students' reaction to the housing shortage showed administrators just how much the world had changed since 1942. Cloyce Box and the other postwar students were a different breed. They were older and more confident. They had seen the world. Some of them had watched men die. They were not easily intimidated. They were not as tolerant or patient as the adolescents who went off to war in 1942. They were in a hurry to make their marks in the world and were not afraid to take matters into their own hands when things didn't go their way.

As a solution to the housing problem, former soldiers slept in the gym on army-style double-decker cots brought in from a former Italian prisoner of war camp just south of Hereford in Deaf Smith County. The college also set up a series of wooden barracks, transported from army and defense facilities all over the panhandle, on several acres of open ground to the west of Buffalo Stadium and flanking the highway. Forty-five travel trailers served as married students' quarters and were snatched up as fast as they became available.[9]

There were weddings every weekend. The justice of the peace was busier than a bootlegger on New Year's Eve.

The High Plains baby boom was off and running.

"Canyon was a lot of fun in those days," L. Louise Box *remembered. "The campus was crowded with young people. The war was over. We were happy to be young and alive. Just about every week one of the dorms had a dance. And when the Box brothers arrived, all eyes were on them. They may have been poor country boys, but they always looked like a million bucks. They wore pressed white shirts. They were big, good looking guys. When they walked into the room, you might not know them, but you wanted to."*[10]

5

Like a Rifle Shot

A successful coach needs a patient wife, a loyal dog, and a good quarterback, not necessarily in that order.

—Bud Grant

Football was king in West Texas, except in Canyon where in recent years West Texas State football played second fiddle to the more prestigious and more colorful basketball team. And yet, the Buffalo football program had its moments of glory and managed to produce a few stars with the talent to play in the National Football League.

Foster Watkins, a quarterback from Memphis, Texas, played for the Philadelphia Eagles in 1940 and 1941, and Orrin Thomas "Tex" Mooney, a 6'5", 280-pound tackle, played for the Cleveland Rams and the Brooklyn Dodgers in 1942 and 1943. There was even a set of athletic twins, Earl and Myrl Goodwin from Paducah, Kentucky, who played for the Buffaloes in the 1920s and with the Pottsville (Pennsylvania) Maroons in the early days of the NFL.

But the attitude around Burton Gym was that football was an inferior game. "The football team was way beneath us then," Cloyce recalled.[1]

Besides, real athletes played basketball. A football player could get by on strength or speed, but basketball required real athleticism and a range of skills.

While the basketball team basked in the national limelight, the Buffalo football team, with a record of 4-3 in 1944 and 2-6 in

1945, had an uphill climb to be average. In 1946, Gus Miller, who coached the basketball team and the football team during the war years, and his assistant Windy Nicklaus, were desperate to turn the football program around and went on the hunt for athletic talent. They didn't have far to look.

One evening Coach Miller and Coach Nicklaus walked over to Buffalo Courts to have a talk with two tall marines who just returned from the war. Cloyce and Boyce Box were natural athletes, and the coaches persuaded the Box twins to play football that fall, probably out of respect for Gus Miller more than anything else. Coach Miller, after all, was responsible for them coming to Canyon in the first place.

"When I came out of the service," Cloyce explained, "Things had changed. Baggett was snarled in a political tangle and basketball slumped. I lost interest and so decided to try my hand at football." Although the Box twins were big, fast, and athletic, when it came to football, they had a lot to learn. "Do you know," Cloyce once asked, "I never saw a game of football until I was eighteen years old?"[2]

Still, when the news hit the street that the Box twins would join the football team, everyone expected them to be stars on the gridiron as well as the basketball court, and Cloyce once said he tried out for the football team "just to prove them wrong."[3] At that effort he was a miserable failure. Years later, Cloyce and Boyce joined Eugene "Mercury" Morris, Duane Thomas, Jerry Don Logan, Terry Funk, and Dory Funk Jr. as members of the West Texas State Athletic Hall of Champions.

Despite Cloyce's athletic talent, his first efforts at West Texas State football were less than sterling and hardly newsworthy. The college listed him on the 1946 depth chart as a second-string halfback, but he got little playing time and rarely made the papers. Boyce, always the better athlete, was the starting left end, but he was clearly disillusioned with the game by the end of the 1946 season. In 1947, Boyce concentrated on basketball and baseball and never played football again.

Cloyce, too, almost quit the football team in frustration after a tumultuous season and a player rebellion that contributed to an unprecedented midseason coaching change. Had Cloyce not returned for the 1947 football season, his life story could have had a much different ending.

The cause of the player rebellion had its roots in the disruption of daily life during the war. In 1942, Jack C. "Cactus Jack" Curtice, the popular Buffalo football coach, left Canyon to become head football coach at the Texas State School of Mines and Metallurgy in El Paso (today UT El Paso).[4] To fill the job vacated by Coach Curtice, West Texas State promoted Curtice's assistant, Leslie Van Meter from Kentucky, to the position of head football coach in January 1942, but Van Meter was called into military service just four months later.

Gus Miller, hired as Van Meter's assistant in February 1942, coached both football and basketball that season. With Coach Van Meter in the army and enrollment low, West Texas State fielded no football team in 1943. Miller coached the football team and the basketball team again in 1944 and 1945.

When the war ended in 1945, West Texas State began a search for a football coach who could return the program to respectability after a string of mediocre seasons, and in 1946 the school chose Winfred "Windy" Nicklaus as the new head football coach.

Coach Nicklaus, who served as Gus Miller's assistant since 1942, had a strong resumé and appeared to be a perfect fit for the job. He was a native West Texan, a graduate of Amarillo High School, the captain of the first Golden Sandstorm football team, and the first team captain of the Texas Tech Matador football team. He was a class officer and a scholar at Amarillo High School and at Texas Tech, graduating in 1928.

Before taking the assistant's job in Canyon, Nicklaus coached at the public schools in Tahoka and Amarillo. He coached Amarillo College to the state junior college football championship in 1935. His other head coaching assignments included Altus (Oklahoma) Junior College, Shawnee (Oklahoma) High School, Oklahoma Baptist University, and Borger (Texas) High School before taking the job of assistant coach at West Texas State in 1942. Later in life, he would become the first principal at Amarillo Palo Duro High School, a civic leader in Amarillo, and one of the most respected men in the Texas panhandle.

But it is unlikely that his tenure in Canyon would make his list of fondest memories. Coach Nicklaus had a rocky start at West Texas State, and it went downhill from there. By accepting the head-coaching job in Canyon, he landed in a firestorm, not of his own making.

The first predicament arose when Leslie Van Meter, who had just been released from military duty, suddenly appeared in Canyon in the spring of 1946 expecting his old job back. It was customary and patriotic for businesses and institutions to rehire veterans to positions held before the war, although, in many cases, there was no contractual obligation to do so. In this case, the college had recently named Coach Nicklaus as head football coach and asked Coach Van Meter instead to take a position as assistant football coach, assistant athletic director, physical education instructor, and swimming coach. With no other immediate prospects, Van Meter accepted the offer but could not hide his unhappiness with the arrangement. The situation had disaster written all over it.

To say that Coach Nicklaus and Coach Van Meter got off on the wrong foot is an understatement. The two men never had a good relationship, and everyone knew it. As the season wore on, Coach Van Meter felt he was not given a voice in handling the team and that "material has not been employed to the best advantage and that his [Van Meter's] coaching knowledge has not been given reasonable range."[5]

Coach Nicklaus believed that Coach Van Meter was secretly fostering discontent among the players. By September, the two men barely spoke to one another.

Then Al Baggett, a civilian again and recently reappointed to his position as Buffalo athletic director, sided with Van Meter, and proposed to the College Athletics Council that Coach Nicklaus be released and Coach Van Meter be restored to the position he held before going off to war. The Athletics Council stuck by its guns, overruled Baggett, and supported Windy Nicklaus as the head coach.

The football team was caught in the middle of this sticky situation, but many of its members, especially certain athletes who returned to Canyon after serving in the military, knew Coach Baggett and Coach Van Meter before the war and took sides with them against the newcomer Coach Nicklaus, the Athletics Council, and the administration.

As the season got underway, game day performance reflected the disharmony off the field. The Buffaloes lost their first three games to Texas Tech, Houston, and New Mexico, although on September 21, 1946, they almost pulled off an upset of archrival and heavily favored Texas Tech in the season opener in Lubbock. Coach Nicklaus could take some satisfaction in a close game against a very good football team. Tech would beat Texas A&M by a score of 6-0 the following week.

Boyce Box was a bright spot against Texas Tech. One reporter wrote that Boyce "played brilliantly both on offense and defense at his end position."[6]

But one good effort on the field did not mean that the drama was over. Although the players stayed above the controversy in the beginning, the hostility between the coaches, intensified by losing, eventually became an issue on the field.

Then in October, a group of older players, unhappy with Coach Nicklaus and partial to fellow veteran Van Meter, asked to meet with Coach Van Meter at his home. The coach granted the players an audience, and they aired their concerns in the coach's living room.

When Coach Nicklaus heard about the meeting, he confronted his assistant and accused Van Meter of dividing the team and fostering discord among the players. Coach Nicklaus also accused Coach Van Meter of planting a story in the Amarillo newspaper that made reference to "alleged dissension on the squad."[7]

Coach Nicklaus, angry with Coach Van Meter and frustrated with his players, called a team meeting to air all concerns. The meeting took place on Friday, October 11, 1946, at the field house, with all the coaches and players present.

At that meeting, some of the players expressed their support for Coach Van Meter and declared their intention to boycott the game against Colorado College on Saturday if Windy Nicklaus remained in charge of the team. Cloyce Box's role in the rebellion is not known because the names of the players who spoke out that day were never made public.

Facing a mutiny, the Athletics Council met in an emergency session on Saturday morning and removed Nicklaus as head coach, replacing him with Gus Miller, but an apparent partial victory for the players backfired when at the same meeting, the council fired Leslie Van Meter and Al Baggett after both men refused reassignment.[8]

That night the Buffaloes beat Colorado College 13-12 in Canyon for their first win of the season. Boyce Box caught several passes. Cloyce rode the bench most of the night.

The frustrations of an entire season were almost erased on November 15, 1946, when the Buffaloes upset the heavily favored University of Wichita Wheatshockers in a wild game in Canyon.

The Shockers held a 6-0 lead in the fourth quarter with the Buffaloes driving for the tying score. An interception halted the Buffalo drive at the Wichita 10-yard line, but Boyce Box stole the ball back from the player who made the interception. After officials gave the ball to the Buffaloes, an argument and then a brawl broke out on the field. It was quite a while before officials separated the teams and restored order.

When play resumed, Buffalo tailback W. N. Reimers carried the ball to the 1-yard line. On the next play, R. A. Boyter smashed across the goal line but was hit so hard the ball came loose. Boyce Box fell on the ball in the end zone for the tying touchdown. Junior Melton kicked two extra points to win the game. The first one was erased when both teams, still fuming from the earlier play, jumped offsides.

When the Buffaloes kicked off, the Shockers completely lost their composure. Blocking and tackling continued long after the whistle. The referee penalized the Shockers half the distance to the goal for unsportsmanlike conduct. Both benches emptied, and the fight was on.

The Buffaloes won the game 7-6, but hard feelings caused a termination of football relations between the two schools. The next year's contest between the Buffaloes and the Shockers, already on the schedule, was cancelled by mutual consent. The two teams didn't play again until 1960.[9]

The experiences of the season had calmed the player rebellion but did not suppress it entirely. The following week when the

Buffaloes played in El Paso, some of the players told Coach Curtice of their intent to transfer from Canyon to El Paso at the end of the current semester. Coach Curtice wisely counseled against it.

"Go on home and forget about it," he said. "Things will be straightened out."[10] That conversation, along with Gus Miller's patience and understanding, eventually suppressed the insurrection.

The team lost its first three games under Windy Nicklaus, but under Gus Miller, the Buffaloes were a respectable 5-2. William Augustus Miller was a pleasant, jovial, and dignified man who helped the West Texas State athletic program survive two crises: a world war and the player rebellion of 1946.

The following year, West Texas State hired the man to lead the Buffaloes out of the football wilderness. His name was Frank Kimbrough, the older brother of Texas A&M All-American fullback Jarrin' John Kimbrough. Frank Kimbrough was a star athlete at Haskell High School and at Hardin-Simmons University. He coached Amarillo Junior College to the Texas State Junior College Football Championship in 1931 and 1932.

Hardin-Simmons University hired Kimbrough, just thirty-one years old, as head football coach in 1935, and under Kimbrough, the Cowboys became a football powerhouse. In Kimbrough's six seasons in Abilene, Hardin-Simmons was 47-8-3, including a 7-1-1 record in 1939 and an undefeated season in 1940. In those years, Hardin-Simmons, a small, private institution in the wilds of West Texas, had one of the most successful college football programs in the country.

In 1941, Kimbrough went to Baylor, but resigned in 1946 after a frustrating tenure at one of the smaller schools in the mighty Southwest Conference. The ink on his letter of resignation was barely dry before West Texas State signed him to a contract. Kimbrough was back in West Texas where he belonged.

After the turmoil of the 1946 season, Cloyce Box had no desire to play football again, but Frank Kimbrough, who was a very persuasive man, had plans for the tall ex-marine. The coach had watched Cloyce's athleticism and smooth ball handling on the basketball court, and saw the makings of a T-formation quarterback.

As the two men got to know one another, their friendship grew. Kimbrough was a tough man, and there was no nonsense about him. He never sugarcoated anything. He was the kind of man Cloyce respected.

"He was a strict disciplinarian as a coach," Cloyce once said about Kimbrough. "One thing you didn't want to happen was to be one-on-one with him. He wasn't an easy touch."[11]

Kimbrough usually got what he wanted, and after what must have been an interesting conversation, Cloyce agreed to come out for the football team.

With the full confidence of his coach, Cloyce progressed rapidly at his new position. His speed and agility were unusual for a man his size and his passing improved every week. Soon *The Amarillo Globe-News* raved about his accuracy and described his passing as "like a rifle shot."[12]

Still, no one expected much from the Buffaloes, and as football season got underway, the lack of faith seemed well placed. West Texas State began the season with three losses (Tulsa, Abilene Christian, and Texas Tech). The defense played well most of the time, but the offense was inconsistent.

Then in game four, Cloyce Box and the Buffaloes caught fire. The team reeled off four wins in a row, including three shutouts. Over those four games, West Texas State scored 111 points (just under 28 points per game) and allowed just one touchdown.

It was during that streak that Cloyce Box's name as a football player first appeared in the national press. In game nine, Cloyce scored two touchdowns and rushed for 130 yards against Colorado College. West Texas State won the game 40-6.

The team ended the season with a record of 7-4, finishing in third place behind Border Conference Champion Texas Tech and runner-up Hardin-Simmons. Frank Kimbrough re-established his reputation as a successful football coach, while Cloyce Box concluded that he might have a future in football.

Meanwhile, there was basketball to fill the cold winter months and by the first of December, Cloyce had joined the basketball team. Despite a late start, he had not lost his touch. In an early game against Arizona State, Cloyce came off the bench to score 14 points in 12 minutes. His outburst carried the Buffaloes to a 46-36 victory.

Later that season, West Texas State had an epic battle with the Arizona Wildcats, the 1948 Border Conference basketball champions.

The Wildcats roster included Fred Enke Jr., who would one day throw touchdown passes to Cloyce Box in Detroit, and Morris K. Udall, a future fifteen-term Arizona congressman.

In March, the Buffaloes earned a trip to the 1948 National Association of Intercollegiate Athletics postseason tournament in Kansas City, Missouri. In the first round, West Texas State beat Wisconsin Eau Claire 71-47 but lost the next game to Nevada. In the next round, Nevada lost by two points to eventual champion Southern Illinois.

But it was Cloyce Box's dominant performance on the football field that made the biggest news beyond the plains of West Texas. Cloyce was certainly an impressive sight, even standing still. He stood 6 feet 4 inches and weighed 220 pounds; he was a big man with world-class speed. He ran a 9.6 hundred-yard dash.[13] Only a handful of men in the known world could run that fast.

Even though Cloyce was a relatively unheralded player from a small college, his size, speed, and athleticism caught the eye of George Preston Marshall, the owner of the Washington Redskins of the National Football League (NFL), who was looking for an eventual replacement for an aging Sammy Baugh. The Redskins picked Cloyce in the 1948 NFL draft (round 20, number 178) after his junior season.

Cloyce Box had barely heard of the Washington Redskins or the NFL, but he went to their training camp in California just to see if he could make the cut. Because he still had a year of college eligibility left, Coach Kimbrough asked for special permission from NFL Commissioner Bert Bell for Cloyce to attend training camp. Kimbrough was covering his bases. If Cloyce proved to be an NFL-caliber athlete, he could sign a contract with the Redskins. If not, he could return to West Texas State to play his final season of college football.

"Heck, I didn't know what the NFL was," Cloyce declared when he learned from an Amarillo sports writer that he had been drafted by Washington, "but I went to the Redskins' training camp at Occidental College and made the team."[14]

Even then, Cloyce was no typical jock. Professional football didn't impress him at all.

"The day before our first scheduled exhibition game, I decided to go back to West Texas. I had another year of eligibility left, and I wanted to work on my masters' degree." Some of his teammates tried to talk him into staying, but when Cloyce Box made a decision, no one could change his mind.

"They still had Sammy Baugh and Harry Gilmer," Cloyce explained, "so I didn't have much of a chance."[15]

"So I went back to Canyon and played football another year for Kimbrough, and in December I entered Baylor Law School."[16] It was Kimbrough with his connections in Waco who advised Cloyce to enroll at Baylor.[17]

The announcement that their star player would be back for another season at West Texas State was a shot in the arm for Panhandle football fans. That year, the Buffaloes finished 6-5. Texas Tech repeated as Border Conference Champions.

Gene Mayfield from Quitaque, who later became a West Texas coaching legend (Littlefield, Borger, Odessa Permian, Levelland, and West Texas State), played quarterback behind Cloyce Box that year. Mayfield felt all along that Cloyce was a natural wide receiver and tried to convince Frank Kimbrough to move Cloyce to that position, conveniently opening up the quarterback position for himself. Mayfield told Coach Kimbrough, "Put that big guy [Cloyce] out there and let me throw to him."[18] Kimbrough never acted on the suggestion, but events to occur later made Gene Mayfield look like a prophet.

While Cloyce was honorable mention All-Border Conference quarterback in 1948, Boyce was the unanimous choice for captain of the basketball team his senior year. The following spring, Boyce graduated and signed as a free agent to play baseball for the New York Yankees.

The Yankees saw his natural athletic ability and assigned Boyce to the Beaumont Exporters, their affiliate in the Texas League. Although Boyce played center field in college, the Yankees turned him into a right-handed pitcher. He had a good curve ball and could throw heat. Then he developed bursitis in his pitching arm and left the game, but not before he pitched two summers for the Amarillo Gold Sox in the Texas League. He also starred on a local

Amateur Athletic Union basketball team. Had he played college basketball a few years later, he would likely have been a high draft choice in the National Basketball Association.

In 1950, Boyce married his college sweetheart, L. Louise Pugh from Perryton. The marines called him back into service in 1951, and he was honorably discharged a captain later that year. He was the athletic director at Abernathy, Texas, for three years where he coached football, basketball, and track.

Boyce spent the next 40 years as a businessman in Amarillo. He built motels (Travel Lodge and Rodeway Inn), mobile home parks, restaurants, and truck stops along Route 66 and Interstate 40, and he sold a million dollars' worth of insurance for Massachusetts Mutual Life Insurance Company.

Meanwhile, Cloyce graduated from West Texas State in December 1948 with a business degree. Confident in his academic abilities, he took his law school entrance exams that fall. He married his college sweetheart the previous year, and she moved with him to Waco in January for his first semester at Baylor Law School.

It was the beginning of a long, bumpy ride.

Fern Virginia Cunningham was born in Malvern, Arkansas (near Hot Springs) on January 23, 1926. She went to elementary school in Hope.

Everyone who knew her talked about her beauty and her grace. "My mother was a beautiful woman," her son Tom Box remembered. "More beautiful than a movie star. My father couldn't help being attracted to her. She was well-read. She loved art and classical music. She played clarinet in the West Texas State band and sang alto in the A Capella Choir. She was a devout woman. Her father was a Methodist preacher."[19]

Fern's father, Sam Cunningham, did many things to support his family during the depression. He farmed, worked for the Santa Fe Railroad, and preached at a small country church. He was an Arkansas state representative, and he delivered the mail. His $40 a week salary as a mailman was enough to give Fern piano lessons.

During the war, Sam went back to work for the railroad, and soon the company transferred him to the Texas Panhandle. Fern graduated from Friona High School in 1944 and earned a business degree from

West Texas State in 1948. She was tall and beautiful, and all the boys in Canyon wanted to date her.

She met Cloyce Box in a business law class (they sat across the aisle from each other), and they soon were inseparable. The most beautiful girl on campus was destined to marry the handsome football star.

They eloped on a Saturday, June 14, 1947, a few weeks after Fern's graduation, and were married by a justice of the peace in New Mexico. Cloyce was a restless twenty-three year old war veteran who came up the hard way. Fern was a naïve twenty-one year old who had been shielded from the hard facts of life by her family and her faith.

Fern believed in fairy tales. Cloyce believed in himself. He was lusty, ambitious, worldly, and had a roving eye. Fern believed a girl fell in love and lived happily ever after and was not prepared for what was about to come her way.

Sam Cunningham was furious when he learned his daughter had eloped. He sent Cloyce the bill for Fern's senior year tuition.[20]

6

The Bomb Squad

There is winning, and there is misery.

—Bill Parcells

While Cloyce Box was in his first semester at Baylor Law School, the Washington Redskins sold the rights to him as a player to the Detroit Lions. The Lions were not very good and were looking for help anywhere they could get it—even from a little known quarterback from a small West Texas college.

What was the going rate for a twentieth rounder in 1948? Detroit paid $250 for the rights to negotiate with the big guy from West Texas State.

At first, Box was not interested in a National Football League contract, but soon changed his mind when he saw that playing professional football made sound financial sense. On the practical side, he could make a good salary playing professional football in the fall and still have the springtime free to study law.

"I got into football because I needed a job," Box once said. "I was going to law school and wanted to buy a house, and I knew I could always out-run everybody. I came to realize that I had an asset in the way of speed."[1]

But Box wasn't all in until he got a call that summer from Detroit Lions head coach Bo McMillin. The coach, who was not in the habit of calling rookies, asked Box to come to training camp.

"I didn't have anything else to do at the moment," Box remembered, "so I said I'd report."[2]

On June 4, 1949, the *New York Times* announced that the Detroit Lions had signed two new quarterbacks: Cloyce K. Box of West Texas State and Steve Nemeth of Notre Dame. Box was a rookie while Nemeth, signed as a free agent, was a member of the Cleveland Rams championship team of 1945.[3] Those events were lost in the other news that spring.

In January, Joe DiMaggio signed with the New York Yankees for $100,000 a year—the first baseball player to earn six figures. With his raise, Joltin' Joe made as much money as Harry Truman—an indication of the growing star power of sports celebrities. Another Joe, Joe Louis, retired in February after a boxing career that included a twelve-year reign as world heavyweight champion and twenty-five successful title defenses—the most in history.

In an early version of March Madness, Adolph Rupp's Kentucky Wildcats beat Hank Iba's Oklahoma A&M Cowboys for the National Collegiate Athletic Association (NCAA) Basketball Championship. After the season, an NCAA investigation implicated Kentucky's Alex Groza (brother of NFL Hall of Famer Lou Groza) and two Wildcat teammates in a points shaving scandal.

In April, *South Pacific* (with Mary Martin as Nellie) opened on Broadway, Jimmy Demaret won the Masters golf tournament by two strokes, and the Minneapolis Lakers, led by feisty 5'10" guard Slater Martin, beat the Washington Capitals in the Basketball Association of America (BAA) finals. The tallest players on the Laker squad were Hall of Famer George Mikan (6'10") and Ray Ellefson (6'9"), Cloyce Box's former teammate at West Texas State. The next year the BAA became the National Basketball Association.

That spring, manager Leo "The Lip" Durocher assaulted a fan after a frustrating 15-2 New York Giants' loss. In May, Polaroid sold its first camera, and the Berlin airlift began. In December, the Philadelphia Eagles, led by Hall of Fame coach Earle "Greasy" Neale and Hall of Fame running back Steve Van Buren, won the NFL Championship.

Television stations were popping up all over the country like Johnson grass in a West Texas cotton field. Ten million American homes had televisions in 1949, and the number grew by the hour. Television would change the world, and the world of professional football, forever. Cloyce Box, the poor boy from Jonesboro, Texas, was in the thick of it.

Luck and good timing followed Cloyce Box most of his life, and his entry into the NFL was no exception. Thanks to television, the popularity of professional football was on the rise. Players were becoming celebrities. Salaries were moving up.

Even the timing of his arrival in Detroit was fortunate, although it didn't seem so at the time. In the late 1940s, no professional sports organization needed a boost more than the Detroit Lions of the NFL.

There was little optimism in training camp at Eastern Michigan University in Ypsilanti that summer. Morale was low. Detroit was horrible—the worst team in the league. The franchise won just one game in 1946 and was 3-9 in 1947. The Lions were 2-10 in 1948 and finished dead last in the Western Division.

The 1949 season, Cloyce Box's first as a professional, started badly. The team lost the first four games and seven of the first eight. Detroit would finish the season with a record of 4-8. This year, like the fourteen before, the Lions had to buy tickets to see a championship game.

Still, Box was happy to be in a place where he got paid to play ball. Professional football was the perfect part-time job. "Coach (Bo) McMillin, who liked Texas boys, got me in a trade," Box recalled. "McMillin was coaching the Detroit Lions. I played halfback some and worked at quarterback."[4] Meanwhile the Lions struggled through another dismal season.

Although it was not obvious at the time, the lowly Lions had begun to turn the corner. In the 1948 draft, Detroit took Les Bingaman, a tackle from Illinois; Fred Enke Jr., a quarterback from Arizona; and Don Doll, a running back from the University of Southern California. Box and Fred Enke had battled each other in college, while Box and Don Doll, both ex-marines, became the best of friends.

For a brief moment, the Lions held the rights to Y. A. Tittle, a quarterback and a future Hall of Famer from Louisiana State University, but traded the rights to negotiate with him to Los Angeles. (Tittle signed with the Baltimore Colts of the All-American Football Conference.)

Over in Philadelphia, the Eagles drafted Lou Creekmur, an unheralded tackle from William and Mary, then traded him to Detroit. Creekmur came from nowhere to have a Hall of Fame career.

In Pittsburgh, the Steelers drafted Bobby Layne, a quarterback from the University of Texas, in round one, but traded him to Chicago. Layne played with the Bears for a year and then with the New York Bulldogs. The Bulldogs folded in 1951, sending Layne to Detroit where he and Cloyce Box would make history.

Meanwhile, the Lions' coaching staff tried to figure out what to do with Box. He had great talent, but no one was sure where he fit.

"They made me a halfback," Cloyce said, "and I probably was the worst halfback in the history of the league. I played a little defense, learned the plays and generally just fooled around. McMillin was a great believer in wind sprints. That was right down my alley. So, I won most of the sprints."[5]

At halfback, Box had 30 carries for 62 yards (2.1 average), but his pass catching was an eye-opener and a surprise to his coaches and the rest of the league.

On November 13, 1949, against the Chicago Bears, the unknown rookie from West Texas State caught two 35-yard touchdown passes from quarterback Frank Tripucka. The Bears won the game 27-24, giving the Lions their seventh loss in eight starts, but Box had found his place. He finished the year with 15 catches for 276 yards (18.4 average—one of the highest in the league). Four of his catches went for touchdowns (fifth in the league). One touchdown catch covered 43 yards. Box also returned three kickoffs for a total of 50 yards (16.7 average).

But it was his high number of yards per catch that convinced his coaches to move him to wide receiver in 1950, and there he would make his mark as one of the very best in the NFL. Gene Mayfield had been right about him all along.

Box was in favor of the move. It fit his practical philosophy of the game.

He was a natural at that position. His straight-line speed was equal to anyone in the league. He had great hands, and he was tall. He towered over defensive backs, and he was impossible to defend in single coverage.

Then in the off-season, the Lions made more changes that would one day make them champions. In 1950, Detroit drafted Doak Walker, an All-American running back from Southern Methodist University. The next year, the Lions signed Bobby Layne, and overnight the team was competitive. Box liked Bobby Layne from the beginning, although their personalities were very different, and the two men had an uncommon chemistry on and off the field.

Everyone liked Doak Walker, including Cloyce Box. Both men had an engineering background, but it was their mutual interest in the business world that was the beginning of a lifelong friendship. Box was obsessed with business. He and Walker spent long hours on road trips discussing ways to make money and laying plans for future business deals.

But more important for the Detroit franchise, Layne, Walker, and Box assumed leadership on the field and in the locker room. These three men and the roles they played, as much as any other factor, would turn the Lions from bottom-feeders into the class of the NFL.

Meanwhile on the football field, a friendly rivalry sprang up between Box and Walker. "George Wilson (McMillin's assistant) almost created the slot back for me," said Box. "Doak Walker and I switched off and on. He'd play left end and left half, then I would."[6] After some early experimentation, the 1950 starting lineup was set with Walker at halfback and Box at wide receiver. It was a decision that would one day carry the Lions to the NFL Championship.

Box was immediately productive at his new position. On a Wednesday night exhibition game at the Cotton Bowl in Dallas against Sammy Baugh and the Washington Redskins, he caught two touchdown passes from Bobby Layne.

On Wednesday, Box was completely unknown. The next day, coaches around the league were wondering "Who is this guy, Box, and where did he come from?"

Just before kickoff that Wednesday night in Dallas, Box called home and learned that Fern, who was 9 months pregnant, had gone to a Dumas hospital in labor. Box played the entire game, jumped in a borrowed car, and hurried to Dumas to see his wife and new son. He and Fern named him Don, after Don Doll. Cloyce and Fern would have four sons and all would carry the middle initial "D" in Doll's honor—another testament to Box's loyalty and the depth of his friendship. On Saturday, he flew from Amarillo to Little Rock to rejoin his teammates for a weekend exhibition game against the Philadelphia Eagles.

Bobby Layne and Doak Walker were established stars in college, but the sports world at large had never heard of Cloyce Box. All that changed with his performance in the 1950 regular season opener. He came out of nowhere and caught a 50-yard touchdown pass that helped his team beat the Green Bay Packers 45-7. During week four, Box grabbed a 23-yard touchdown pass from Layne as the Lions beat San Francisco 24-7. He caught a 34-yard touchdown pass in game five and a 58 yarder the next week. Cloyce Box was suddenly getting a lot of attention.

But it was on November 23, 1950, Thanksgiving Day in Detroit, that Box became a star. In a nationally televised game, he caught four passes for 123 yards against the New York Yanks. Three catches went for touchdowns of 65, 21, and 17 yards. Bobby Layne threw two of the touchdowns; Fred Enke threw the third. The Lions thrashed the Yanks 49-14.

And Box was just warming up. One week later, in a game in Baltimore with only 12,059 spectators in the stands, Box, described in the press as "an extremely slippery customer," had a monster day. He caught 12 passes for 302 yards and four touchdowns. The touchdown passes, three from Bobby Layne and one from Fred Enke, covered 80, 66, 35, and 28 yards. The Lions beat the Colts 45-21.[7]

His performance that day set NFL receiving records for touchdown catches of at least 20 yards in one game (4) and touchdown catches in a two-game stretch (7).

Cloyce Box joined another elite club that day in Baltimore. At the time, only one other player in NFL history had over 300 yards receiving in a single game. On November 22, 1945, Jim Benton of the Cleveland Rams caught 10 Bob Waterfield passes for 303 yards against Detroit.

By the end of the 1950 season, there was a general feeling around the league that the Lions were a team with a championship in its future. Detroit would finish that year at 6-6—its best record since

1945. The team won three of the first four but had a midseason slump and lost four in a row. Two of those losses were by three points and could have gone either way.

For the first time in years, there were signs of life in the Lion's den. Four members of the team made the Pro Bowl: Walker, Box, defensive back Don Doll, and defensive tackle Thurman McGraw. Not a single Lion had made the Pro Bowl since 1945. Doak Walker was the NFL Rookie of the Year and a unanimous selection to the All-Pro Team. Cloyce Box was a second-team All Pro.

For the season, Box had 50 receptions for 1,009 yards and 11 touchdowns. He averaged just over 20 yards a catch. Almost overnight, he had become a star and a central figure in plans for the future.

But Uncle Sam had different plans. In February 1951, while Box was studying law in Waco, his marine reserve unit was recalled to active duty for service in Korea. He barely had time to pack and notify the Lions front office of his recall. He passed his physical on February 26, 1951, and left the next day by train for Camp Pendleton near Oceanside, California.

Box would spend the 1951 NFL season in service to his country—one of fourteen NFL players to see action in both World War II and Korea. He spent most of his time in the legal division, and he ran a brig for six months. He also played service football with a team from Camp Pendleton, and he learned to fly.

Box returned to the NFL in 1952 and resumed a career that represented an important stage in the evolution of the wideout or flanker. Don Hutson was the first modern wide receiver. Hutson played college football at Alabama (the "other end" was Bear Bryant), and he played professionally for the Green Bay Packers from 1935 to 1945. Hutson was the first of his kind: a speed-burner who ran deep routes and was capable of catching the bomb and scoring anytime from anywhere on the field.

In a time when most professional football teams were run-oriented, Hutson was the first receiver to have more than 50 catches in a season and the first to have over 1,000 receiving yards in a season. He led the league in scoring for five consecutive years—an NFL record. He once caught four touchdown passes in a quarter

(October 7, 1945) and ten touchdown passes in a month (November 1942)—both NFL records. He was a two-time league MVP (Most Valuable Player) and a member of the inaugural class of the Pro Football Hall of Fame.

Hutson's skills and style of play turned professional football on its ear. Defenses tried everything to stop him—man-to-man, zones, double coverage, triple coverage, but no one could contain him for long. Don Hutson was the first star wide receiver in NFL history and the first speedster who was a threat to go downtown on every play. His numbers are still impressive, even in light of today's high-flying offenses.

After Hutson retired in 1945, Tom Fears of the Los Angeles Rams and Mac Speedie of the Cleveland Rams reigned as the premier receivers in the league. For his career, Speedie averaged 800 receiving yards a season and almost 50 receiving yards a game. Fears was technically the first wide receiver or wide out—the first receiver to line up on the line of scrimmage away from the tackle. His productivity, to the tune of 400 receptions for over 5,300 yards led to his selection to the Pro Football Hall of Fame in 1970.

Cloyce Box only played five seasons so he didn't rack up the career receptions or yardage to match Fears or Speedie, but he was a greater scoring threat than either of them. The numbers prove it. Fears had a career-high nine touchdowns in 1949. In eight seasons, he scored thirty-eight touchdowns. Speedie caught seven touchdowns in two different seasons (1946 and 1949). He had thirty-three touchdowns in seven seasons. Box caught eleven touchdown passes in 1950 and fifteen in 1952. He had 32 touchdowns in his five-year career. He averaged a touchdown every 4.03 catches—still one of the best in history.

He relied on his nimble fingers, his height, and his remarkable speed. He didn't run fancy routes, and he wasn't much of a blocker. At the snap of the ball he ran straight down the field.

Yet, Box was a defensive back's worst nightmare. His size and speed made him almost impossible to single cover. When defenders played him tight, he went deep. When defenders played him loose, he caught the ball underneath and was still a threat to score.

"And don't forget," Lions' assistant coach Buddy Parker added, "he [Box] caught very few of them in the end zone. He can run with the ball like a halfback. He was fast and could get out in the open."[8]

In years to come, wide receivers like Don Maynard, Lance Alworth, Lynn Swann, Jerry Rice, Michael Irvin, and Chad Johnson elevated pass catching to an art form, but not before Don Hutson invented the position and Tom Fears, Mac Speedie, and Cloyce Box refined it.

"I was just about the first real wide receiver—at least the way you'd think of them now," Box said in explaining his style of play. "The game was just opening up, but there still wasn't all that much to it. I'd run the same pattern just about every time. I wasn't that skilled a player, but I was fast. Back then, that was about all you really needed to get by."[9]

He was being modest. "He was a hell of a receiver," said Lions Hall of Famer Joe Schmidt. "He was 6 foot 4 and his speed was comparable to any of today's wideouts. He had a graceful stride, and at 220 pounds he was a big sized man."[10]

"I tried to cover him in practice, and he made a better defensive back out of me," recalled Yale Lary, another Lions Hall of Famer. "You wouldn't think he was really that fast, but he ran like a deer and was so large I had to climb all over his back."[11]

Frank Gifford recalled the first time he played against Cloyce Box. "In 1952 the New York Giants played the Detroit Lions in Norman, Oklahoma. I was a rookie, and he had been in the league a few years. I had heard of him. Knew him by reputation. By 1952 everybody knew who he was. He was the most dangerous deep threat in the League."

"For most of the game Cloyce was split out to the right. I played defense on that side, and I was supposed to cover him. Well, I couldn't cover him with a blanket. No one could cover him man to man. He was too fast. He wasn't the greatest athlete I ever saw, but he was so darn fast. He blew past me like I was standing still."

"Early in the game he got behind me and scored on a long pass play. When I came to the sideline my coach Steve Owen, who was known to occasionally use sarcasm, said, 'Playing him a little loose aren't you?'"

"The next week they moved me from defense to offense, so in a way I have Cloyce Box to thank for my career."

"He was so fast that he outran the football. Bobby Layne told me that when he threw deep to Cloyce Box, he took a quick three-step drop and threw the ball as far as he could. Layne said it was impossible to overthrow Cloyce Box. He said no matter how far down the field he threw the ball, Box could run under it."[12]

Cloyce Box was good, and he was surrounded by quality teammates. The Detroit Lions of the 1950s were an exotic combination of exceptional athletic talent and some of the craziest characters who ever broke curfew. The colorful Lions made news, on and off the field. They were tailor-made for the exciting new medium of television.

Halfback Clyde Scott from Arkansas was a silver medalist in the 110-meter hurdles at the 1948 London Olympics. Jim Hardy was an adequate backup quarterback to Bobby Layne, although he once threw eight interceptions in a game against Philadelphia—an NFL record that still stands. In 1953, the Lions selected Joe Schmidt, a center and linebacker from Pittsburgh. Schmidt played his way into the Pro Football Hall of Fame. King-sized middle guard Les Bingaman from Illinois was surprisingly agile for a man as big as a barn. He weighed 350 or 360 pounds, depending on what he had for lunch. His exact weight was a mystery. Most scales topped out at 300 pounds. The rest was a ballpark figure.

The Lions defensive secondary was the best in the business. Yale Lary was a third-round draft choice from Texas A&M in 1952. At free safety, he had fifty career interceptions and made nine Pro Bowls.

Jack Christiansen was born in Sublette, Kansas, the epicenter of the Dust Bowl, and raised in an orphanage before going to Colorado State on a track scholarship. Despite his modest size—6'1" and 170 pounds—he took to the game of football.

Soon after arriving in Detroit, Christiansen became the unchallenged leader of the defensive unit. He was a five-time Pro Bowler and a six-time All Pro. He had 46 career interceptions and was the most dangerous kick returner of his time.

Jim David looked tiny and out of place on the field. He was only 5'11" and weighed 170 pounds, but he packed a wallop. He was a superb pass defender and one of the most feared tacklers in the NFL. Yale Lary and Jack Christiansen made the Hall of Fame. Jim David might have made the Hall had he played on a team with a little less talent.

In 1949, the Lions selected Doak Walker from SMU as the third pick in round one. Doak was smart, handsome, and athletic. He and Bobby Layne started their football careers playing the guard position at Highland Park Junior High in Dallas. It took Layne all season to convince his coaches he could play in the backfield, but in the first game, Walker intercepted a pass and returned it 75 yards for a touchdown. The next day he was a halfback.[13]

Doak was an All-American running back at SMU and the 1948 Heisman Trophy winner as a junior. He was small, only 5'11" and weighed 175 pounds, too small, the experts believed, to survive in the NFL. As usual, he confounded the experts. In his six-year career, he was All Pro five times, and he played a starring role in two championships for the Lions. He was elected to the Pro Football Hall of Fame in 1986.

Gil "Wild Horse" Mains, from Murray State Teachers College in Kentucky, was a 6'3" 260-pound tackle who was testy, surly, and belligerent beyond the call of duty. He was a brawler, on and off the field. He supplemented his regular income as a wrestler in the off-season. His nickname came from an inclination to whinny and snort at the man across the line of scrimmage.

Tackle Lou Creekmur, by contrast, was even-tempered and jovial—the perfect cover for a devious man. Creekmur, who played college ball at William and Mary, was an expert at playing the victim. Beginning with the first play of the game, he slugged, slapped, and poked his opponent when the referees weren't looking, then screamed for justice when the man retaliated. Creekmur seemed so inoffensive and unassuming; the refs always took his side. He smiled and played his part, all the way to the Hall of Fame.

Leon Hart was a three-time All American at Notre Dame and was only the second lineman ever to win the Heisman Trophy as the best college football player in the country—an award that routinely went to high-profile quarterbacks or running backs. He was the number-one pick in the 1950 NFL Draft. Hart was huge—

6'4"and 260 pounds—and yet he had great hands and was surprisingly agile for a man his size.

Harley Edward Sewell was a blond, snuff-dipping farm boy from Saint Jo, Texas. He was 6'1" and weighed 200 pounds. He played fullback and linebacker for the Saint Jo Panthers, and he earned a reputation for speed and toughness that spread as far as Austin.

The summer after high school graduation, an assistant coach for the University of Texas went to Saint Jo looking for Harley and found him atop a telephone pole doing his summer job as a lineman for the phone company. Harley would sign with the University of Texas, but only after vigorous recruiting and extensive negotiations.

"How would you like to play football for the University of Texas?" asked the coach.

"Be fine," Harley answered from his perch at the top of the pole. The deal was struck.[14]

Harley had been to Wichita Falls a few times, but was unprepared for city life in Austin. At first, he was so homesick for his family he refused to unpack, but Assistant Coach J. T. King convinced him to stay. In time, he adjusted to the rhythm of the city. He even sampled the pleasures of Austin nightlife—over and over again.

Although at Texas he was known primarily as a linebacker, the Detroit Lions drafted him in the first round (thirteenth overall pick) as a pulling, trapping guard, and he had the speed and size to do it. He defined the position of pulling guard in the NFL. He made a career blasting holes on the sweep in front of Doak Walker and pass blocking for Bobby Layne.

Layne, the undisputed leader of the Lions, was born in Santa Anna, Texas, but raised by an aunt and uncle in Highland Park. While his friend and high school teammate Doak Walker went to SMU, Bobby played baseball and football at the University of Texas. He was a pitcher for the Longhorns, and in 4 years, he never lost a conference game. He played quarterback on the football team and was an All-Southwest Conference performer all 4 years.

The Chicago Bears got Bobby in the first round, and then traded him to the New York Bulldogs of the American Football League.

The singer Kate Smith owned part of the team, but the organization was not well financed.

"Every time Kate Smith got a sore throat," Bobby Layne used to say, "We worried about getting paid. If she couldn't sing 'God Bless America,' there wouldn't have been any checks."[15]

As it turned out, there was good reason for concern. The team folded after 1 year and Detroit picked him up. Whatever the Lions paid to get Layne was a bargain.

Layne's athletic talent was considerable but may have been eclipsed by his leadership skills. He had a commanding presence and the ability to bend strong-willed men his way. He was noisy, caustic, and dictatorial. When he stepped on the field, no one questioned his orders, and nobody wanted to disappoint him. Off the field he was the life of the party, while on the field he was demanding and confrontational. Players who made mistakes found his huddle a very unpleasant place to be.

"I've seen him chase [teammates] out of the huddle and send them to the sidelines if they missed a block," said Laverne Torgeson, Layne's teammate with the Lions.[16]

His delivery wasn't perfect, and he couldn't throw a tight spiral if his life depended on it. His passes wobbled through the air like wounded ducks. But when the game was on the line, no one was better than Bobby Layne. He was a winner at everything he did.

Dick "Night Train" Lane, the Hall of Fame defensive back, praised Bobby Layne and explained the problems Layne and Cloyce Box caused for opposing defenses. "Unitas was great," Lane said, "but for me Bobby Layne was the toughest quarterback. He'd tire you out. He'd put more in three minutes than anybody. And he had a receiver, Cloyce Box, who could run all day. He'd run deep on you five times in a row. When those two were with the Lions, before I got there, they were tough."[17]

Off the field, Layne was a free spirit who lived hard and fast. He didn't have six-pack abs. He had a beer gut. His drinking escapades and road trips were legendary.

Teammate Yale Lary recalled, "When Bobby said block, you blocked, and when Bobby said drink, you drank."[18]

Laverne Torgeson roomed with Layne, "until about Tuesday each week. He'd have left me far behind by then."[19]

Once when Harley Sewell was a rookie, he went with Layne to get a tube of toothpaste. They didn't get back for three days.

Each year during training camp, Layne staged a drinking contest with the rookies. Bobby retired undefeated.

There are people who insist that Bobby Layne's reputation as a hell-raiser was inaccurate. Cloyce Box was one of them.

"My father always said that the stories about Bobby Layne were all wrong," Tom Box recalled. "Dad said the stories were not even close to how wild he really was."[20]

7

On a Roll

When it's third and ten, you take the milk drinkers and I'll take the whiskey drinkers.

—Max Magee, Green Bay Packers

The player revolt in Detroit in 1951 was strangely reminiscent of the 1946 player insurrection at West Texas State. This time, the rebellion sent head coach Alvin "Bo" McMillin to the front office as general manager and replaced him with a slow-talking West Texan named Raymond "Buddy" Parker.

The move was popular for at least two reasons. Everyone liked Buddy Parker, and almost no one, at least among the players, liked Bo McMillin. In fact, a group of players from Texas used brazenly their star power to bring about his removal from the sidelines. The episode was a glaring example of the way celebrities, made famous by television, were changing the world of professional sports.[1]

The grumbling among the players began at training camp in 1950 when McMillin, an old-school coach who was a stickler for the rules and who demanded punctuality, fined Leon Hart $25 when Hart was late for a team meeting. McMillin's tough management style served him well as a college coach at Kansas State and Indiana, but was not well received by the temperamental TV stars in the professional ranks.

Bobby Layne fell out with McMillin because the coach tried to stop the players from drinking, smoking, and carousing. Layne was an adult, and vowed he would have a drink anytime he wanted. Then there was a disagreement over the play-calling system. McMillin insisted on calling all plays from the sideline. Layne wanted to call his own plays in the huddle.

The problem became a crisis when McMillin tried to curb the social activities of some of the star players. Members of the Lions' board of directors liked to hang out with celebrities and often invited the stars on the team, like Layne, Walker, Box, and Hart, to parties and other social events. Coach McMillin put a stop to such treatment "because of the deteriorating effect it had on the less famous players. If you want to invite the whole squad," McMillin reasoned, "that's OK, but you can't play favorites."[2]

That decision seemed fair and reasonable, but did not take into account a new reality. The stars were no longer just football players. Television had made them celebrities with a new kind of star power that often trumped a coach's authority.

While the players complained, Coach McMillin doubled down. For him, it was "my way or the highway."

In the old days, most players would have remained quiet and miserable, but the younger generation, who had lived through depression and the war, was not afraid to challenge authority. Many of them freely expressed their unhappiness to the press. The discontent had a noticeable effect on team performance.

The low point came on October 29, 1950, when the Rams embarrassed the Lions 65-24 in Los Angeles. Something had to be done.

The Lions organization held a closed meeting of players, coaches, and management on December 18, 1950, one week after the season ended, to explore solutions. There had always been speculation that Box was a leader in the West Texas State field house rebellion of 1946. In Detroit, Box was one of the clubhouse leaders, and everybody knew it.

"There are some giant egos in professional football," Frank Gifford explained. "The Detroit Lions of the 1950s had some of the largest egos in the world. Nobody could intimidate those guys. Bobby Layne and Doak Walker had the biggest egos of all, but even they had great respect for Cloyce Box. Bobby Layne and Doak Walker were superstars. They didn't listen to many people, but they listened to Cloyce. I think they were intimidated by his intelligence. They were better athletes than Cloyce, but they were in awe of him."[3]

At the meeting, Layne, Walker, and Box took control of the situation. They stepped forward and bravely expressed dissatisfaction with Coach McMillin and his "handling of certain personnel issues."[4] The meeting ended with no action taken, but Lions' management was on notice that something needed to be done.

Then in January, Layne, Walker, and Box announced to the press that they would no longer play for the Lions if McMillin remained as head coach.[5] Six players had originally come forward in opposition to the coach, but three feared for their jobs and backed down.[6] Still the choice was clear, and when given the option of keeping their coach or their star players, Lions management backed the players.[7]

Within days, the front office reassigned Bo McMillin to general manager and promoted assistant coach Buddy Parker to head coach; something Layne, Walker, and Box probably wanted all along.

A short time later, the Lions paid off the remaining $60,000 on McMillin's $90,000 three-year contract and dismissed him from the organization.[8] That summer, he took the job as head coach of the Philadelphia Eagles, coached the first two games of the 1951 season (both wins), and then died of a heart attack at age 57.

Buddy Parker, born in Slaton, Texas, on the high plains south of Lubbock, was just the breath of fresh air the Lions needed. He drank beer with the players and didn't interfere with their social lives. He understood that superstars played by a different set of rules. He was a good coach, but he stayed in the background and let his players shine.

His laid-back style endeared him to his players. Cloyce Box, Doak Walker, and Leon Hart liked Buddy Parker. Parker understood Bobby Layne and let Bobby call his own plays.

With harmony restored, the Lions began to look like champions. Led by a brash group of Texans, there was a newfound confidence in the Detroit locker room, and on the field there was a swagger not seen since the Lions of old, led by the great running back Dutch Clark, beat the New York Giants for the NFL Championship in 1935.

This time, the team started slowly, but gained momentum as the season wore on. After losing two of its first three games of the 1952 season (both losses to Y. A. Tittle and the San Francisco 49ers), Detroit won the next five straight and eight of the next nine. The team finished the season with a record of 9-3, tied with the Los Angeles Rams for the lead in the Western Division of the NFL.

That season, Cloyce Box enhanced his reputation for making big catches in important games. He was always a threat to catch the bomb, and he became the most feared wide receiver in professional football for his ability to turn a game around with a single reception. Bobby Layne, who handed out compliments like glasses of water at happy hour, declared Box to be the best pass receiver with whom he had ever worked.[9]

Old-timers in Detroit still talk about two touchdown catches Box made on October 19, 1952, that propelled the Lions into the playoffs for the first time in seventeen seasons. The game was in Detroit against the Los Angeles Rams—the defending champions of the NFL. At the time, Detroit was a team with potential, but not yet a bona fide contender. The playoffs were a long shot, thanks to recent uninspired play and several losses to inferior teams.

The Lions' offense had been inconsistent and ineffective. Prior to the Rams' game, Detroit had not scored a point since Cloyce Box scored a pair of touchdowns two weeks earlier.

When the Lions failed to score in the first quarter against the Rams, the crowd of 40,152 could contain itself no longer. Impatient fans showed their displeasure with boos and catcalls. At the beginning of the second quarter, they threw trash on the field.

Then Cloyce Box went to work. "You know that second touchdown catch looked tough," he recalled. "Actually it was easy to dive forward and get that one. The first long toss over my head was the tough one to catch."[10]

"If there was a turning point," Coach Buddy Parker said about the game and the season, "that [Box's first touchdown catch] was probably it."[11]

Before Box worked his magic, it looked as if the Rams would

crush the Lions who continued a familiar pattern of dismal play. Then Box scored his first touchdown, a 64-yard catch and run at 13:05 of the second quarter after the Rams had jumped out to a 13-0 lead. Embarrassed by the boos coming from the stands, Box raced straight down the field, past two defenders, and took the ball over his shoulder in full stride. The throw was a wobbler and almost out of reach, but he caught the ball on his fingertips, bobbled it, then pulled it in and sprinted into the end zone. It was the Lions' first touchdown in 126 minutes of play covering three games.[12]

The second scoring play came in the third quarter with the Rams ahead 16-14. The Lions reached the Ram 10-yard line after speedy Jack Christiansen's 65-yard punt return and a 22-yard pass from Bobby Layne to big Leon Hart. On the next play, Box slipped into the back of the end zone from his position on the wide side of the field while Bobby Layne handed the ball to fullback Bob Hoernschemeyer on a reverse. Hoernschemeyer faked the run, and then raised his arm and threw a low bullet into the end zone. Box dove between two defenders to make the catch just as he hit the turf.[13]

That touchdown gave Cloyce Box four of the five Lions' touchdowns for the season. More important, the Lions won the game. Detroit now had a record of 2-2 and was in a second-place tie with Green Bay and Chicago in the Western Division—two games behind unbeaten San Francisco.

And Box was just warming up. He caught a touchdown pass against the Steelers in game seven and a 64 yarder against Dallas the following week.

Then, in the final 3 weeks of the regular season, Cloyce Box went on a tear with an historic barrage of receptions and touchdowns. On Thanksgiving Day, the Lions ripped Green Bay 48-24. He had six receptions for 116 yards, including touchdown catches of 5, 33, and 4 yards.

On December 7, 1952, Box made two over-the-shoulder circus catches for touchdowns as the Lions pounded the once mighty Chicago Bears 45-21. Just two weeks earlier, the Bears had upset the Lions 24-23 after George Blanda threw the winning touchdown pass to Ed Sprinkle with nine seconds to play.

On this day, the Bears could not contain Cloyce Box and Bobby Layne. Box had 8 receptions for 172 yards and 3 touchdowns.

The next week against the Dallas Texans, Box had 7 receptions for 202 yards, including touchdown catches of 77, 41, and 40 yards. The Lions crushed the Texans 41-6.

In those three games, Box had 21 receptions for 490 yards and 9 touchdowns. It remains one of the most productive streaks by a wide receiver in the history of the NFL.

Detroit was on a roll. The win over the Rams in game four lit a fire under the Lions and propelled them into the playoffs. With the momentum of a freight train, Detroit won seven of the next eight games and finished the season in a tie with the Los Angeles Rams for first place in the Western Division.

A lot of credit goes to Cloyce Box. A reporter described the way Box's presence on the field could influence a game. The Rams, "knowing Box was the big threat as a receiver, spotted three defenders on him. Layne threw a couple to big Leon Hart; he hit Bill Swiacki with a few more; he sent Pat Harder and Hunchy Hoernschmeyer through and around the line. And then when the defense around Box was forced to loosen up, Layne went back to Box as his receiver."

"Even so the winning touchdown was scored by Box after he raced down the field with a three-man cover, turned and literally dived toward his own line of scrimmage to catch a pass on which the defenders didn't have a chance to intercept."[14]

On December 21, 1952, the Los Angeles Rams and the Detroit Lions met in a playoff at Briggs Stadium in Detroit before 47,645 fans. The stadium was wrapped in fog. The marquee matchup of the game was to be Cloyce Box against Dick "Night Train" Lane, but Train was injured and didn't play.

"The loss of Lane is probably the most severe loss we could sustain," Rams coach Hampton Pool said. "He was our one chance to stop Cloyce Box."[15]

Box presented such a threat from his position at wide receiver that the Rams devised a special plan to stop him. The *New York Times* reported that Hampton Pool "is working on a plan to shift Elroy (Crazy Legs) Hirsch, an offensive end-halfback (and future

Hall of Famer), into Lane's vacant spot in the hope that Hirsch could cover Detroit's sensational end Cloyce Box."[16]

The Rams paid so much attention to Box that other players could not be covered. After the game, a sportswriter wrote "also important in an unspectacular way was Cloyce Box who caught 15 touchdown passes in the 12 previous games—four of them against the Rams. Box caught only two passes but constantly drew two or three defenders after him and that opened the way for other pass receivers."[17]

Teams could defend the old Lions by ganging up on a single star player, but this was a new Lions team with too many weapons to focus on one man. In this game, the bruising fullback Pat Harder stepped up in a big way, carrying the ball 8 times for 72 yards and 3 touchdowns. He also kicked 4 extra points and a 43-yard field goal. The other touchdown came when Bobby Layne handed the ball to Doak Walker in what looked like a sweep right. When the defenders rushed up to make the tackle, Walker threw a 24-yard bullet to Leon Hart standing all alone in the end zone. The Lions beat the Rams 31-21 and earned the right to play for the championship of professional football.

On December 28, 1952, a sellout crowd of 50,934 watched the championship game between the Lions and the Browns at Cleveland Municipal Stadium. The DuMont Network televised the game coast to coast to those Americans with televisions. Harry Wismer was behind the microphone.

The NFL feared that people within driving distance of Municipal Stadium would watch the game on television for free rather than pay to see it, so the Cleveland market was blacked out. Browns fans in and around Cleveland had to buy a ticket or drive to another city to see the game.

In years to come, the NFL would learn not to fear television but embrace it. Television, in turn, would make professional football the most popular sport in America and turn franchise owners into billionaires.

Cloyce Box had a quiet afternoon in the championship game, but the Browns so respected his abilities that he influenced the game without catching a pass.

The Lions stuck to their game plan and ran the ball all afternoon. Bobby Layne threw only nine passes, but the Browns had two defensive backs watching Box all day just in case he might get loose in the secondary. The Browns' preoccupation with Box opened up the running game for the Lions.

The play of the game came in the third quarter with the score tied 7-7. Box lined up wide to the left, and two defenders followed him to that side of the field. Bobby Layne took the snap and handed the ball to Doak Walker who shot through the left side of the line before cutting back to his right. The two defenders with Box on the wide side of the field were out of position and unable to make a play. Walker went 67 yards for a touchdown.

Doak got the headlines, but Cloyce Box got a Lions' share of the credit from the coaches. "Box was the guy who made Doak Walker's touchdown run possible," Assistant Coach Aldo Forte told reporters in the locker room.[18] The Lions beat the Browns 17-7. It was their first championship since President Franklin Delano Roosevelt's first administration.

The irony of the game was that the Browns dominated in every statistical category but points scored. Cleveland had twenty-two first downs to the Lions' ten. The Browns racked up 434 yards in total offense to Detroit's 258. Cleveland's Otto Graham completed 20 passes for 157 yards while Bobby Layne completed only 7 for 59 yards. The Browns had 227 rushing yards to Detroit's 199.

Still, the 1952 championship game brought fame and fortune to a franchise that was more than ready for it. The mojo had returned to the Motor City. A celebration of fans in Detroit spilled out into the streets and turned into a riot. Season ticket sales spiked. Bobby Layne partied for a week, sobered up, and partied some more.

Five Lions from that team made the Associated Press All-Pro Team: Bobby Layne, Cloyce Box, defensive tackle Thurman McGraw, offensive guard Lou Creekmur, and defensive halfback Jack Christiansen.[19]

For the year, Box had 42 receptions for 924 yards. He averaged 22 yards a reception, and he scored 15 touchdowns, a Lions record until Calvin Johnson broke it in 2011. Cloyce had become the premier pass receiver in the NFL.

Box also finished second in league scoring with ninety points.

Gordy Soltau of the 49ers finished first with ninety-four points, and Lou Groza of the Browns finished third with eighty-nine. Box held the top spot until the last weekend of the season.

By early January, Box was back in Waco. He spent his days studying law and his evenings at the library. When the F5 tornado hit Waco at 4:36 on the afternoon of May 11, 1953, Cloyce, Fern, and their two young sons lived near the Baylor University campus and were spared the destruction that destroyed much of downtown and killed 114 people.

Buddy Parker made one attempt to curb Bobby Layne's evening activities, but the effort backfired like an old pickup truck. One Saturday night, Parker persuaded Bobby to stay out of the bars and go to bed early. The next day, Bobby played horribly, and Parker, famously superstitious, never tried that tactic again.

"Kid's had a highball in his hand since he was 14," Parker told a reporter after the disaster. "It was no time to change him."[20]

8

Bigger Fish to Fry

Pro football is like nuclear warfare. There are no winners—only survivors.

—Frank Gifford

Most professional athletes take life at a slower pace in the off-season, but Cloyce Box picked up the tempo. In January, he and Fern were back in Waco with son Don, age 2, and infant son Gary. Fern took care of the house and the children while Cloyce studied law and looked for ways to make money.

That spring, Cloyce and Doak Walker began buying real estate in the booming North Texas market. Within a few years, the money Box made from real estate would cause him to lose interest in professional football.

In the meantime, Nick Kerbawy, the new Detroit Lions General Manager, flew to Dallas to talk contracts with Cloyce Box and the other stars from Texas. Kerbawy signed Doak Walker to a 2-year deal and reached terms with Bobby Layne, but found Cloyce Box "cool" to the Lions' offer.[1] Although the Lions didn't know it at the time, Box was also talking to the Winnipeg Blue Bombers about jumping to the Canadian Football League.[2] It was all about money.

There was a time when Winnipeg could have gotten him cheap. In 1951, Box wrote a letter offering his services to the Blue Bombers after talking to Buddy Tinsley, a Winnipeg tackle, who played college ball at Baylor and lived in Waco in the off-season. At the time, Box's offer did not even generate a response, and the matter died.

Now Box was a star, and this time, Winnipeg Coach George Trafton took no chances. He immediately mailed Box a contract with a nice salary figure already filled in. Winnipeg wanted him and believed it was free to negotiate with him because he didn't play that year (he was in the marines) and was therefore a free agent.

Then a small scandal erupted when a Canadian sportswriter contacted a Detroit newspaper seeking a picture of Box to go with a story of his impending signing by the Blue Bombers. When the Detroit newspaper told the Lions' front office that Winnipeg was negotiating with its star wide receiver, the Lions' attorney filed an injunction.

Then in June, before the whole matter went to court, Box signed a 2-year deal with Detroit that made him one of the highest paid receivers in the league. The Winnipeg controversy didn't hurt his bargaining position. Cloyce Box was not yet a rich man, but he wasn't poor white trash any more.

On August 14, 1953, the Lions, representing the National Football League as champions, played the College All-Stars in a charity game at Soldier Field in Chicago before 93,818 spectators and millions more watching on television. The Lions won the game 24-10. In the third quarter, Bobby Layne connected with Cloyce Box on a 48-yard pass play. A few plays later, Layne hit Box again for a 9-yard touchdown. The All-Stars never stood a chance.

"This is one of the best pro teams I've seen," declared Bobby Dodd of Georgia Tech, coach of the All-Stars. "We knew Bobby Layne could throw, but we didn't count on such outstanding receiving. Leon Hart made two great catches on us, and that Doak Walker and Cloyce Box were terrific."

"I don't think we were ever in the ball game although that long pass that Layne threw to Box was the key play," Dodd added.

Lions coach Buddy Parker agreed. "When we moved the ball the way we did I was sure we could take them. Bobby Layne's passing and our catching were great."[3]

News reports said Bobby Layne wasn't feeling well that night (could have been a hangover from the night before), but no one could tell from his performance. The quarterback tore apart the

All-Star defense completing 21 of 31 passes for 323 yards. He made it look easy.

The hype surrounding Cloyce Box gave the Lions an edge before the game even started. The All-Stars was so geared to stop the deep aerial attack that they left themselves wide open across the middle.

"They concentrated on not letting our receivers get behind them," Layne explained, "and there was nothing to do but pass in front of them."[4] The Lions were ahead 24-3 halfway through the fourth quarter and cruised the rest of the way.

Several weeks later, the Lions played the New York Giants in an exhibition game before 37,000 fans at the Cotton Bowl in Dallas. Cloyce Box was in usual form catching two touchdown passes as the Lions trounced the Giants 38-7.

Then on October 18, 1953, Box hurt his leg in a game against the Rams. The coaches listed him as a starter the next game against the San Francisco 49ers, but the injury dogged him the entire season. For the first time in his career, productivity fell off dramatically. Robbed of his blinding speed by a bum leg, he caught only 16 passes for the season for 403 yards (25.2-yard average) and 2 touchdowns.

But even at half speed, Box would still make magic. On November 26, 1953, at Briggs Stadium in Detroit, the Lions trailed the Packers 15-7 at halftime. A crowd of 52,607 and millions more on national television watched the Lions play sluggish and uninspired football. Then an electrifying catch by Cloyce Box turned the game and the season around.

"It was a bad day in Detroit," Box recalled. "It was Thanksgiving morning. Green Bay was kicking us all over the field."

"Bobby (Layne) had a bad case of bursitis, and our passing attack wasn't working at all. Bobby Dillon was covering me and you know what a great defensive back he was."

Then on a play late in the game, Dillon apparently turned his knee.

"Dillon definitely had hurt himself," Box said. "He's not the kind of guy you could beat, but if you keep trying long enough, somehow you manage to do it once or twice."

"We were on our two or three-yard line. Layne must have been five yards back in the end zone when he threw this one. I caught it at our 40, and I was clear all the way."[5]

Bobby Layne described the play for reporters. "Leon Hart ran an over pattern deep enough to get behind the linebackers. Cloyce Box ran a 'post,' splitting the cornerback and the safety. The pass puts a lot of pressure on the right safety, especially if they doubled up on our flanker—Doak Walker—with strong coverage."

"Because Box was so fast and usually took both defensive men with him, Hart (a big man and quite a bit slower than Box) was usually open. If the safety saw Hart coming across and dropped off, Box was open."

"Against Green Bay that day, the safety man spotted Hart coming across and picked him up. Box beat the cornerback and was wide open for a 97-yard score. This got us back in the game and we won easily, 35-14."[6]

That scoring play was only Box's second touchdown of the year, but was a factor in saving the season and the Lions' title hopes.

The next week, Box had 2 receptions for 110 yards as the Lions beat the Packers 35-24. Detroit finished the year with a record of 10-2 and earned another trip to the championship game.

On December 27, 1953, 54,557 fans watched the Lions and the Browns play again for the NFL Championship. Millions more watched the action, described by Harry Wismer and Red Grange, on the DuMont Television Network.

The Browns had some unresolved issues from the year before, and from the beginning, this game was a tough and bloody affair. Players tangled on the field, and there were several brawls that cleared the benches. Neither team played well. In three quarters of play, Bobby Layne had found the end zone only once. Layne's counterpart, the meticulous, efficient, and future Hall of Famer Otto Graham, had an awful game—completing just 2 of 16 for 20 yards.

Thankfully for Cleveland, Lou Groza's toe was working just fine. Groza kicked three field goals, Chick Jagade scored a touchdown, and with three minutes to play, Cleveland was ahead 16-10. Detroit had the ball deep in its own territory. Only a miracle could win the game for the Lions. The conditions were ideal for the birth of a legend.

Bobby Layne drove his team through the doom and gloom in Detroit's Briggs Stadium, working the clock to perfection. On that day, he invented the 2-minute drill and capped it off with a dramatic 33-yard touchdown strike to end Jim Doran, subbing for the injured Leon Hart. With the game tied, Doak Walker kicked the extra point to give the Lions a 17-16 victory and their second NFL Championship in a row.

Lions' fans were still celebrating when rumors of Box's retirement began. For the year, he averaged a career high 25.2 yards per reception, but his nagging injury and low number of catches, not to mention his growing business interests in Texas, fueled rumors that he might turn in his uniform. But Buddy Parker was optimistic that his star wide receiver would return in 1954 better than ever.

"He's as fast as he ever was," said Parker. "We think he'll make a good comeback."[7]

For Box, there was a lot to consider. By 1954 he was spread thin. He and Doak Walker owned a Buick dealership in Belton, and he had real estate developments underway in Fort Worth and Killeen. He owned a home-building company in Garland, and he was buying tracts of land near Paris, Texas, and along the shores of Lake Texoma.

Box was starting to make big money away from football. Each year, he ran the numbers in his head to see if it made sense for him to make training camp.

For now, the numbers didn't quite add up, but the time was fast approaching when professional football would not be worth the time he devoted to it.

On August 13, 1954, the Lions played the College All-Stars at Soldier Field in Chicago. The All-Stars, coached by Jim Tatum of Maryland, had four excellent young quarterbacks: Zeke Bratkowski from Georgia, Cotton Davidson from Baylor, Bobby Garrett from Stanford, and Vince Dooley from Auburn.

A crowd of 93,470 packed Soldier Field to watch rookie quarterback Tom Dubinsky lead the Lions to victory. The record attendance, along with the nationwide television audience, made the contest the most watched sporting event in history.

Then on September 19, 1954, in a 48-23 win over the Chicago Bears, Box injured his leg again. Although he started the next game 2 weeks later against the Rams, he never fully recovered and watched most of the season from the sideline. Even with their deep threat out of commission, the Lions finished the 1954 season 9-2-1, including a 14-10 victory over the Cleveland Browns in the final regular season game.

On December 26, 1954, the Lions and the Browns played for the NFL Championship for the third year in a row. Over 43,000 fans packed Cleveland's Municipal Stadium, and they were not in a good mood. If the Browns lost to the Lions again, things could get ugly.

The sellout was a surprise considering the Browns only sold 24,000 tickets in advance. The DuMont Television Network televised the game coast to coast, except for the blacked out Cleveland market. Millions more heard the broadcast on the Mutual Radio Network, with Chris Schenkel at the microphone.

With the Lions leading 3-0 in the first quarter after a Doak Walker field goal, the Browns punted from deep in their own end of the field. The punter got the ball away a fraction of a second before Harley Sewell ran over him like a diesel colliding with a white tail deer. Officials called the Lions for roughing the kicker, giving the Browns a first down at the Lions' 35. Two plays later, Browns' quarterback Otto Graham hit Ray Renfro for a 37-yard touchdown pass. The fat lady started warming up.

Otto Graham gave a Hall of Fame performance that afternoon. He had been muzzled in the last two championship games, but not today. He ran for three touchdowns and passed for three. Bobby Layne threw forty-four passes, but could only manage a lone touchdown.

The final score was Browns 56 Lions 10, the second-most lopsided score in NFL Championship history after the 73-0 blowout by the Bears over the Redskins in 1940. The 1954 championship game was the first time in nine tries that the Browns had beaten a Buddy Parker coached team.

On April 6, 1955, general manager Nick Kerbawy flew to Dallas and had lunch with Cloyce Box, Doak Walker, and E. D. Walker, Doak's father. Cloyce drove up from Belton where he and Fern had a home close to his Buick dealership and his real estate interests in Killeen. The Lions' general manager was encouraged by the talks and announced afterward that he felt Doak would play another season. Kerbawy was not so certain about Box but stated that he intended to mail Box's contract to him later that summer and was hopeful Box would sign it.[8]

Coach Buddy Parker was less optimistic, stating that Box, "who is doing all right in business in Texas and may retire at any time."[9]

Sure enough, that summer Box notified the Lions front office that he was retiring from professional football to give his full attention to his burgeoning business career.

Professional football was a whistle stop for Cloyce Box. Everyone knew he was on his way somewhere else.

His friend Frank Gifford summed it up. "It was no surprise when he retired. Football was a sideline job for him. We all knew Cloyce Box had bigger things to do than play football. He had bigger fish to fry."[10]

For most athletes, retirement from professional sports is the end of the most exciting time of their lives, but for Cloyce Box the adventure was just beginning.

Grave of R. D. Box Sr. King Cemetery. Photo by author.

Grave of R. D. Box Jr. Cloyce had the headstone made to honor his father. It is the biggest and boldest tombstone in King Cemetery. Photo by author.

P. T. Lemmons, Jonesboro superintendent and basketball coach, was like a father to the Box twins. Courtesy Jonesboro ISD.

Buffalo Courts at West Texas State. The first dorm for athletes in Texas. It was the most luxurious living quarters the Box brothers had ever seen. Courtesy Special Collections in the Cornette Library at West Texas A&M University.

Cloyce Box in basketball pose. "The football team was way beneath us then." Courtesy Special Collections in the Cornette Library at West Texas A&M University.

"Buffaloes, hell, they're giraffes." The Buffalo basketball team playing to the media. Cloyce Box #26. Boyce Box #27. Courtesy Special Collections in the Cornette Library at West Texas A&M University.

Cloyce Box in track pose. He could run like a scalded dog. Courtesy Special Collections in the Cornette Library at West Texas A&M University.

Coach Gus Miller. A pleasant, jovial, and dignified little man. Courtesy Special Collections in the Cornette Library at West Texas A&M University.

Coach Frank Kimbrough. There was no nonsense about him. He never sugarcoated anything. Courtesy Special Collections in the Cornette Library at West Texas A&M University.

Cloyce Box. Not yet comfortable in his football uniform. Courtesy Special Collections in the Cornette Library at West Texas A&M University.

Cloyce Box. His passing was like a "rifle shot." Courtesy Special Collections in the Cornette Library at West Texas A&M University.

West Texas State Buffaloes just before a flight to Tempe, Arizona, in 1947. This was the first team flight in history for West Texas State. The Box brothers are on the right in matching double-breasted suits—the first suits they ever owned. Courtesy Special Collections in the Cornette Library at West Texas A&M University.

Cloyce Box, #24, on the loose against Colorado College. Courtesy Special Collections in the Cornette Library at West Texas A&M University.

Cloyce and Boyce Box in 1948. "When they walked into a room you may not know them, but you wanted to." Courtesy Special Collections in the Cornette Library at West Texas A&M University.

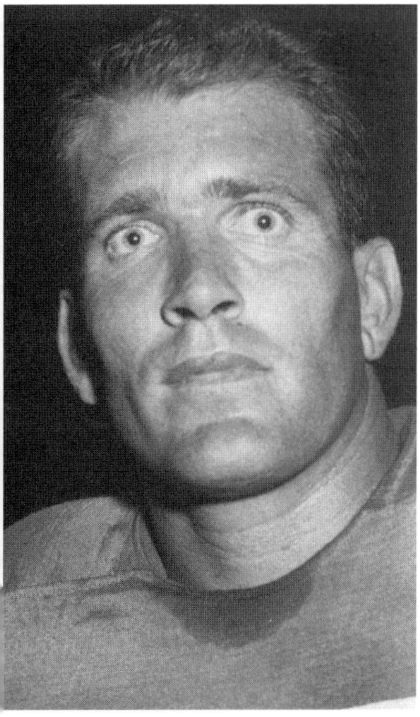

Cloyce Box. Detroit Lions.
Courtesy AGN Media.

Cloyce Box at work. Courtesy AGN Media.

The Snake River Trip, 1969. The families of Cloyce Box, Boyce Box, Frank Gifford, Boots Adams, Frank Cannon, and guests pose by the aircraft just after landing in Idaho. Courtesy Gary Adams.

Cloyce Box at OKC Corp. Six-feet-four and bulletproof. Courtesy AGN Media.

Cloyce Box in a lighter moment.
Courtesy AGN Media.

Chairman of the Board.
"I never invite trouble,
and I never run from it."
Courtesy AGN Media.

Cloyce Box. Lost in thought. Courtesy AGN Media.

Cloyce Box. He kept his troubles to himself. Courtesy AGN Media.

Cloyce Box. Still a great presence, but his magnificent body was beginning to show its age. Courtesy AGN Media.

9

A Robust Cycle of Prosperity

As long as you are going to be thinking anyway, think big.

—*Donald Trump*

Cloyce Box was always looking beyond the end zone. Even as an active player, Cloyce Box had a reputation as a businessman of unusual ability. He was consumed with business. His knack for starting businesses and making money amazed his friends and teammates in the National Football League—many of whom came to him for financial and career advice.

Cloyce was always looking beyond the end zone. One early business was a used car lot in Belton. Then in 1954, Cloyce, brother Boyce, and Doak Walker bought the Buick dealership at 301 North Penelope in Belton and brought in Cloyce's marine buddy, Frank Cannon, to run it.[1] Cloyce once sold eleven new Buicks in one day—the largest sale by a single dealer in the history of Buick's drive away program.[2]

Cloyce wasn't afraid to try anything he thought would turn a profit. He and Walker built a twenty-four-lane bowling alley in Midland, and they were state distributors for plastic bags.[3] The two men had an interest in a 229-unit housing development in Killeen—a tiny hamlet in the cedar brakes between Belton and Lampasas, until the establishment of Fort Hood, the largest military training facility in the western world, brought thousands of soldiers and turned this village in the middle of nowhere into a real estate boomtown. Box and Walker were also partners in a

165-unit subdivision (Shady Oaks) in Paris, Texas, and a 520-acre resort community called Tanglewood Hills on Lake Texoma.

Football and business weren't always a good mix, but Box and Walker made it work. They couldn't play football forever and had to think about the future. In those days, no one got rich playing professional football.

During the season, the two men often flew to their weekend destination ahead of their teammates to have meetings, and they had to carefully budget their time in order to take care of business both on and off the field. The problem was that each year, business took up more of their time and attention, leaving less for football.

"We're supposed to eat at four and rest until kickoff," Walker said one hectic football weekend in Dallas, "But I've got to make a personal appearance at 4:15 at E. M. Kahn & Co. (clothiers that handled Doak Walker personally designed slacks), and I've got a lot of calls to make."[4]

Doak could get away with such things because television had made him a celebrity. He played by a different set of rules than the other players. There were always rumors going around that Doak was about to retire anyway.

"He has to," Box told a sportswriter. "He can't get the time to play football anymore."[5]

While Bobby Layne and other legendary hell raisers of the NFL prowled the bars, partied until dawn, and gambled away large sums of money, Cloyce Box read the *Wall Street Journal* in his hotel room and prepared for the day he would leave the game for good. He kept up with the news in London, Tokyo, Hong Kong, and New York. Nothing escaped his attention. Almost everything that happened in the world affected American commerce, and to be prudent in business, he had to keep up with it all.

Box was a man for his time, with talents, skills, and attitude that meshed perfectly with the economic atmosphere of postwar America. More than anything, he wanted to get rich, and he couldn't have picked a better time for it.

In the 1950s, the American economy was on fire, ignited by a perfect storm of financial optimism, high demand, high employment, higher wages, and cheap money. These were the golden years of American business. A smart and aggressive businessman with a friend at the bank could make a pile of money while still young enough to enjoy it.

Every statistic was encouraging. In 1946, the population of the country was 140 million. Then soldiers returned from the war and got busy. By 1966, the population of the United States was 200 million. So, in a way, the postwar economic boom was driven by sheer numbers. More people meant more of everything—more cars, houses, food, toilet paper, and toothbrushes.

Accompanying the rise in population was a relatively low unemployment rate (typically less than 5%) and an overall increase in personal disposable income that boosted consumer spending. Congress raised the minimum wage to $1 an hour, giving Americans more spending power. In the 1950s, the average worker earned twice as much income in forty hours as a worker in 1900 earned in sixty hours. Average weekly earnings rose from $24 to $44 in the 1950s. Americans had discretionary money to spend on products manufactured by factories that hired still more workers to make still more stuff in a robust cycle of prosperity.

The upward spiraling economy, jump-started by wartime manufacturing, yanked the country out of depression and positioned America for the great economic boom of the 1950s. Americans went on a shopping spree. Many items once considered luxuries, like cars, televisions, transistor radios, refrigerators, gas stoves, electric irons, washing machines, and record players, were now necessities. The manufacturing sector could see no end in sight. Financial optimism was at a level never seen before. The gross national product doubled between 1950 and 1966.

Home ownership soared, boosted by easily obtainable Veterans Administration and Federal Housing Administration loans and by the restructuring of mortgages by lending institutions in order to stimulate the housing market after the war. In the 1930s, mortgages came with high down payments and variable rates. Terms were five to ten years. Homeowners typically renegotiated their loans every year.

After the war came 30-year mortgages with low fixed rates—typically 4% or under—with low down payments. At the same time, William Levitt, a New York real estate developer, first applied mass production techniques to home building, forcing costs down and helping make homes affordable to millions of young couples. For the first time in history, owning a home was within reach of most families.

As a result, Americans in record numbers moved from the inner cities and from rural areas to new single-family dwellings in suburbia. Private residential construction amounted to $1 billion in 1945. One year later, the figure was $6 billion. In 1950, the value of residential construction was $18 billion. In 1960, the value was $29 billion. Each year, the housing boom created thousands of new real estate millionaires.

The automobile fed the proliferation of suburbs. The wide-open spaces of America had already created a passion for automobiles, and that passion, pent up by the Depression and World War II, exploded in an almost irrational excess in the 1950s. There were 31 million registered cars and trucks in the United States in 1945. The number rose to 49 million in 1950 and to 56 million in 1953. For General Motors (GM), the year 1955 was historic. That year alone, GM sold 8 million new cars and rose to the top of the Fortune 500 list. By 1965, the number of registered cars and trucks had risen to 90 million.

Automobile financing came of age in the 1950s. Car loans were easier to get. As a result, the number of families that owned cars doubled. The General Motors Acceptance Corporation financed 4 million cars in 1928. By 1958, that number had climbed to 40 million. Car dealerships in the hands of good businessmen were guaranteed moneymakers.

During the war, Americans had saved their money like never before. There was nothing to spend it on.

But now, exciting new products and sophisticated television advertising caused a buying frenzy that created a dramatic and unprecedented economic boom—the greatest period of sustained economic growth in the history of the world.

The raging economy unleashed a near perfect business environment. "Made in America" was the world standard for quality. Businesses of all sorts raked in the money, hand over fist.

Businessmen were becoming wealthy in unprecedented numbers. The foundations for many great fortunes were laid in the 1950s. Any businessman worth his salt was at least a millionaire before the age of forty. If an entrepreneur couldn't make a million dollars in this environment, he wasn't worthy of the title.

There were 3,000 millionaires in the Unites States in 1944. By 1965, there were 50,000. Cloyce Box was destined to be one of them.

"I don't know if he would call it destiny," his friend Maurice Campbell said, "but he really believed he was born with unusual gifts that set him apart from ordinary men. He believed he was special. He believed he was destined to do great things."

But fate was not the only factor in the equation. The events of his childhood prepared him for his career in the business world.

"I've pondered this a lot," Campbell said, "and I believe Cloyce was motivated to succeed by a number of things. He was raised in terrible poverty, and he never wanted to be poor again. He liked money and the things it could buy. To him money validated his success. It was proof that he was somebody."

"And his mother was a big influence in his life. He loved her very much and wanted to please her. He wanted to give her all the things that she couldn't afford when she was young. She sacrificed a lot for him, and he wanted to repay her."

"But more than anything, Cloyce had a natural talent for business. He was smart. His mind worked in interesting ways. He had an unreal ability to figure things out. He was always thinking ahead. He had a forceful, compelling personality and unusual leadership skills. And of course he was super competitive. He couldn't stand to lose at anything. His childhood in Jonesboro taught him to stand tough and that hard work was a way of life. If you didn't work you starved. No one ever accused Cloyce Box of burning daylight."

"And he was temperamentally suited for the business world. Nothing rattled him or made him nervous. He was the most level-headed man I ever knew. Very even keel. He never lost his cool. Sometimes his business dealings would have him in four or five lawsuits at the same time. Everybody was snipping at his heels. Millions of dollars on the line. But nothing bothered him. Emotional displays were not his style. He could blow off catastrophes that would crush the spirits of most men."[6]

To go along with his drive to succeed, his coolness under fire, and his intelligence, Box had hypnotic powers of persuasion and an almost magical ability to make friends. He made an instant connection with everyone he met. People who met him never forgot him.

"I liked him immediately," said Kent Hance who met Box when he joined the board of regents at West Texas State University. Hance worked for Governor Preston Smith who made the appointment. Hance would later become a state legislator and chancellor of Texas Tech University.

"Cloyce treated everyone the same," Hance remembered. "He treated the hotel maid the same as the bank president. And he never forgot a name."

"Once Cloyce asked me to go to New York with him. He had tickets to the Knicks/Celtics game at Madison Square Garden."

"We flew to New York in his Saberliner; then took a limo to his place at the Excelsior Apartments on 57th Street in Manhattan. When we arrived, the doorman said 'Hello Mr. Box.' Cloyce called the doorman by his first name. Cloyce then called the desk clerk by his first name. He called the elevator operator by his first name. The elevator operator thanked Cloyce for helping his son get a job."

"Cloyce made every person he met feel special."

"And he was a generous man. He sometimes left $100 tips."

"But he also had a type A personality," Hance continued. "He projected strength. It started with his physical appearance. He was a big man. His size could be intimidating."

"At the office there was no question who was in charge. His employees didn't argue with him. He would listen to people, but once he decided on a direction, that was it."[7]

Box's friend and attorney Norman Smith described him as "a gifted man. He was hands down the best salesman I ever saw."[8]

Although Box sometimes appeared to be shy, he had a narcissistic personality that craved attention. He was in constant need of affirmation, and he got it from all sides. Everyone he met fell under the spell of his personality, treated him special, and competed for his esteem and affection. It was a problem men of enormous personal magnetism just had to live with.

"My father was eloquent and charismatic," Tom Box explained. "He just had a way with people. He could get anyone to like him at the drop of a hat. That may have been his greatest talent. People were drawn to him."[9]

Cloyce Box used his powerful personality to charm his way into the most exclusive boardrooms in America, and his circle of high-flying friends would one day include American presidents, foreign dignitaries, Latin-American dictators, heads of state, CEOs of Fortune 500 Companies, celebrities, jetsetters, and the richest and most powerful men and women on earth. He did business with the Rockefellers. He belonged to the same Dallas spa as Stanley Marcus, W. O. Bankston, and Nelson Bunker Hunt. Roger Staubach was his friend and business partner. Hillary Rodham Clinton was a stockholder in his company. Former Miss America, television personality, and former first lady of Tennessee, Phyllis George, sat on his Board of Directors. His best friend was Frank Gifford, the iconic athlete and broadcaster. Gifford called Cloyce Box "one of the truly memorable people I met in my life."[10]

Maurice Campbell recalled when Box and Gifford first met. "Years ago opposing NFL teams sometimes stayed in the same hotel. One night after a game against the Giants, Cloyce went downstairs to the bar—Bobby Layne's watering hole. Cloyce didn't drink, but while he was standing there talking to friends, he saw Frank Gifford sitting alone at a table. Frank didn't drink either. Cloyce went over and sat with Frank. The two men struck up a conversation and became friends. It was a friendship that lasted a lifetime."

"Frank looked up to Cloyce, especially Cloyce's abilities as a businessman. Cloyce was his role model, and they spent a lot of time together. Frank sought Cloyce's advice on all kinds of things."

"Once Cloyce, Frank, and their sons went on a vacation to shoot the rapids on the Snake River in Idaho. Frank was still an active player but was toying with the idea of leaving football to become an actor or a sports announcer. He had already been in eight or nine movies and seemed to be moving in that direction."

"Frank asked Cloyce for advice. I don't know exactly what Cloyce told him but not long after that, Frank retired from football and went to work for ABC Sports."[11]

Doug Box remembered the time that "Green Bay played Dallas at the Cotton Bowl in the late 60s, and Frank called the game for television. He invited dad and me to sit behind him in the booth."[12]

"They were close," Maurice Campbell added. "When Frank's son Kyle had a drug problem. Frank called Box for advice, and

Box said, 'Send him to me.' Kyle lived with the Boxes for a while. I think Cloyce may have sent Kyle to work on one of his oil rigs in West Texas just to get him away from everything. Whatever Cloyce did, it worked. At Cloyce's funeral, Frank Gifford credited Cloyce Box with saving his son's life."[13]

"Frank Gifford loved my father," said Tom Box, "and my father loved Frank. They were the best of friends. My father liked Frank because Frank was a genuine guy. He was a celebrity but didn't act that way. They had many adventures together."

"Once dad went to a party with Frank and met John Wayne. Another time they met Muhammad Ali at a restaurant in New York. Frank's face was instantly recognizable all over the country, especially after Monday Night Football. With Frank, you never knew who you might run into. But Frank was a real person. He didn't act like a celebrity. My father appreciated that."[14]

Tom Box recalled another former professional athlete made famous by *Monday Night Football* who came to Cloyce Box for career advice. "I remember the night that Don Meredith came to our house. My father knew Don from the Dallas social circle. They sat in our living room in Frisco and talked about the future. Don told dad that ABC wanted him to do Monday Night Football with Keith Jackson (replaced one year later by Frank Gifford) and some guy named Howard Cosell. He wanted my father's advice on whether or not he should take the job."[15]

Everyone recognized Box's wisdom, intelligence, and superior judgment. "You didn't have to spend five minutes with him to learn he was smart as hell," Frank Gifford said. "He didn't miss a thing. He just absorbed everything around him. I first knew him as an athlete, but what was exciting was to watch him be so successful in another world. There was a fraternity down there in Dallas—Tom Landry, Roger Staubach, Doak Walker, Kyle Rote. That group was very successful apart from football. Cloyce was part of it."

"And he had sex appeal," Gifford added. "He had a country charm that most people found irresistible. Men were in awe of him, and women were fascinated by him. He was so sure of himself, but he was also a little shy. Of course he was tall and handsome. Women loved him for his masculinity. Those qualities were big factors in his success."[16]

Box was keenly aware of his extraordinary gifts, especially his ability to impress people. "Pro football made Cloyce Box a celebrity," said his friend Hugh Aynesworth. "People were attracted to him because he was famous. But he was smart enough to use his star power to make friends with people who could help him succeed in business."[17]

Cloyce Box may have been raised in poverty, but he soon grew comfortable rubbing elbows with the rich and famous. Billy Dyer from Jonesboro told of the time he traveled to Florida with Maurice Campbell. "It was right after Mr. Box died. Mr. Campbell had some business there, and I went with him. We went to Cloyce Box's horse ranch. I remember going into Cloyce Box's office and looking at the pictures on his desk. One picture in particular caught my eye. It was Cloyce and his wife sharing a mint julep at the Kentucky Derby with Donald Trump and his wife. That picture reminded me just how far he had come from a shack in Jonesboro."[18]

Box had indeed made an amazing transformation. As a teenager, he knew he had special gifts, and beginning in college he intentionally groomed himself, inside and out, for the success he was certain would come his way. In manners and appearance, he distanced himself from his childhood home and the coarse world in which he grew up.

He refined his writing and speaking skills and became an avid reader. At Louisiana Tech, he learned to appreciate the order, predictability, and precision of mathematics. He read classical literature, especially Greek mythology, and like Pygmalion, he chipped and polished away the rough edges of his personality. He became an engaging conversationalist on a wide range of topics. He knew how to conduct himself in polite society. He drove a Lincoln Continental, and wore expensive suits and shirts with French cuffs. He didn't use tobacco and he wasn't much for alcohol. (His mother didn't approve.) Because he knew the power of first impressions, he took great pains with his appearance. He was neat as a pin—never a wrinkle in his clothes or a hair out of place.

But at the same time he was a sentimental man, and he never

forgot that much of what he was he owed to his childhood in Jonesboro. Every few months, he called P. T. and Bess Lemmons, and he stayed in touch with the other families that sheltered him when he had no place to go.

"Even after he became rich and successful, Cloyce Box never forgot my parents," Blake Lovelace Jr. recalled. "They took him in when his mother got sick. For the rest of their lives he contacted them periodically, just to see how they were doing."[19]

The people of Jonesboro repaid him with their loyalty. When he had legal troubles, when magazines and newspapers called him a crook, the people in Jonesboro always stood by him.

So much of his life was a puzzle of contradictions not easily explained or understood. He could be aggressive and ruthless at business, but on a personal level, he was mannerly, courteous, and hospitable. He cared about others and was generous with his money. There was a graciousness about him that was hard to balance with his reputation as a square-jawed businessman.

"Cloyce was an amazing friend," Norman Smith remembered. "He was generous to a fault. If he liked you and trusted you, he relied on you. And he would do anything for you."[20]

As his financial empire grew, he acquired all the material things a poor boy from Jonesboro could want. He lived in luxury and had the best of everything. He drove the biggest car and lived in the biggest house. His mansions were often mistaken for Tara from *Gone with the Wind* or Southfork from *Dallas*—except in both cases there was no mistake. He really lived at Tara (a replica from the movie) and at Southfork. He owned a 300-acre thoroughbred farm in Florida, an apartment on New York's trendy Upper East Side, a 2,000-acre ranch near Dallas, and the 2,600-acre Box Ranch between Moody and Waco.

In Texas, a ranch is an aristocratic symbol. Every big shot in Texas has a ranch. Cloyce Box owned two. The Box ranches were trophies and tangible proof that a poor country boy had made his mark in the world.

But even his family noticed that money and success changed him. His sister Wilmuth, who loved him dearly, wrote "He was always so special, before he was rich."[21]

Cloyce enjoyed the country life, but he went to great lengths to insure that no one mistook him for a country bumpkin. Everything he owned and everything he did was big, brash, and overstated. He flew around the country in an Aero Commander until 1967 when he traded it in for a seven passenger Learjet. On the street he drove a white Lincoln Continental, the biggest car money could buy.

And Cloyce's Lincoln had something few other cars had: a car phone. The contraption took up most of the back seat, and the service was hit and miss, but Cloyce didn't care. His Lincoln had a car phone in the 1960s when few other people had one.

That was the point. He enjoyed racing down the street and talking on his car phone while the 8-track stereo played his favorite song: "Make the World Go Away" by Eddy Arnold.[22]

10

The Martini Bowl

Whoever walks with the wise will become wise,
but the companion of fools will suffer harm.

—Proverbs 13:20

Cloyce Box leveraged his position as an athlete and a celebrity to build relationships with rich and powerful people who could help him get what he wanted. Three men in particular mentored Box and gave him his start in business: legendary oil and gas man Oscar Wyatt of Houston; the equally legendary K. S. "Boots" Adams, President and CEO of Phillips Petroleum Company; and Dallas real estate mogul Trammell Crow.

Wyatt, Adams, and Crow, like Box, had "boss" personas and were born to run things. They were poor boys who made good in the boom years after World War II by working 20-hour days and by using their aggressive and engaging personalities to make things happen.

Wyatt, Adams, and Crow liked Box from the start. They included him in their tight circle of friends and invited him into a world few people get to see. They opened doors for him, taught him the ropes, loaned him huge sums of money, and gave him the power to determine his own destiny. Cloyce Box learned to do business by watching, and sometimes copying, these corporate giants at their best and at their worst.

Oscar Sherman Wyatt Jr. was born a poor boy in Beaumont on July 11, 1924, and raised in Navasota, a small Central Texas town hit hard by the Depression. After his father abandoned the family, in much the same way Box's father had abandoned his, Wyatt picked cotton to make ends meet. Picking cotton was a dreadful experience, and Wyatt vowed that one day he would claw his way out of the cotton patch and never go back. The war was his way out.

After graduating from Navasota High School in 1941, Wyatt joined the army air corps and was a combat pilot in the Pacific. The war taught Wyatt that life was fleeting, and when it came to time, there were no guarantees. He became a man in a hurry to make something of himself before his time ran out.

Like so many poor ambitious young men of his age, he returned home after the war and made the most of the GI Bill. In 1949, he earned a mechanical engineering degree from Texas A&M.

Wyatt, like Box, had a huge ego and an indestructible self-confidence. He could stand alone against the world. He was willing to gamble everything he had (and a lot he borrowed from other people) for a chance to get filthy rich.

He worked briefly for Kerr-McGee as a drilling engineer in Freeport, Texas, and then as a salesman for the Reed Roller Bit Company.

However, Wyatt, like Box, didn't have the temperament to work for other people, and in 1950, while selling drill bits in the oil field, Oscar Wyatt hatched a plan to gather and sell unwanted natural gas being flared by oil wells. He hocked his Ford sedan for $800 to start Hardly Able Oil Company, the forerunner of Coastal States Gas Corporation. He soon earned a reputation as one of the toughest, most unpleasant, and most successful negotiators in the business.

By 1963, shares of Coastal States traded on the New York Stock Exchange, and the bombastic Wyatt was a millionaire several times over. That same year, he married Lynn Sakowitz whose family owned Sakowitz department stores. Lynn, a friend of Mick Jagger and Andy Warhol, presided over Houston society for decades.

Meanwhile, Oscar Wyatt conducted business using methods that were often harsh and uncompromising. He eliminated competition by aggressively buying out his competitors. (Cloyce Box would do the same.) Wyatt constructed pipelines and purchased others—sometimes in friendly transactions and sometimes in hostile takeovers. The phenomenal growth of Coastal States came through the acquisition and development of gathering systems that connected gas wells with large transmission lines.

Wyatt was famous for doing business with a heavy hand. In the 1960s, natural gas powered the plants that generated electricity for much of Texas, and in 1962, the Lovaca Gathering Company, a subsidiary of Coastal States Gas Corporation, entered into a 20-year contract with San Antonio, Austin, Corpus Christi, and other South Texas cities to provide their power plants with fuel. At the time, the cities had few options since Lovaca owned the pipelines. The company had a monopoly in South Texas in the gathering and transporting of natural gas.

Oscar Wyatt had the gas and pipelines to move it when no one else did, and his agreement called for the cities to pay 23.75 cents per 1,000 cubic feet of gas with the price moving up to 28 cents at the end of the contract.

The cities thought they were being fleeced.

Then in 1973, the production of natural gas fell off sharply, and the price spiked. Some East Coast cities were paying as much as 82 cents per 1,000 cubic feet. Lovaca, however, was unable to increase its prices because it was locked into an agreement for another nine years. Wyatt asked for a voluntary increase to 48 cents, but the cities turned him down.

Angered by the cities' refusal to grant a voluntary price increase, Wyatt did what few men had the nerve to do. He promptly sold off his reserves to eastern cities at a great profit for himself, and then reneged on his contracts to Austin, San Antonio, and South Texas. In the dead of winter, Lovaca announced it was unable to meet the demand of its customers. Oscar Wyatt turned off the heat to South Texas claiming he did not have enough gas in reserve to "heat dinner."

Schools, colleges, and universities, including the University of Texas at Austin, closed for a time that winter for lack of heat. Electricity doubled in price, and Lovaca became the embodiment of corporate greed. Hotels refused to take Lovaca's credit cards. A disgruntled customer shot out the windows of the Lovaca office in San Antonio.[1]

Wyatt is known for giving millions to charity. He is equally known for acquiring those millions in some of the sleaziest deals in the history of business. He openly traded with Libya, a sworn enemy of the United States, and he was very friendly with Saddam Hussein. He angered the State Department when he and John Connally visited Hussein on the eve of the first Gulf War.[2]

Later, he pled guilty to paying "surcharges" (bribes) to Saddam's Jordanian bank account in order to win contracts connected to the United Nations Oil for Food Program. He spent a year in jail.

Wyatt made another visit to Baghdad just before the second Gulf War in 2007. An employee of the Iraqi State Oil Marketing Organization alleged that Wyatt told the Iraqi government when the second invasion would occur and the size of the attacking force.[3]

"My father and Oscar Wyatt had some dealings early on," Box's son Tom recalled. "But the two men had a mixed history. Dad didn't approve of the way Wyatt did business, and they soon went their separate ways."[4]

The man who had the most influence on Cloyce Box's early business career was Boots Adams. There was a time when Boots Adams and Cloyce Box were like father and son.

Kenneth Stanley Adams Sr. was born on August 31, 1899, the son of a Rock Island Railroad engineer from Horton, Kansas. When Kenneth Sr. was a boy, he received a pair of black leather cowboy boots with red tops as a gift. He refused to take them off, even when he went to bed. He was called Boots ever since.

Boots graduated from Wyandotte High School in 1917 and entered the University of Kansas where he played football, baseball, and basketball. He had a summer job delivering ice in Bartlesville, Oklahoma, the corporate headquarters of Phillips Petroleum, and it was there at a pickup basketball game, Adams had a chance meeting with Bill Feist, a Phillips employee and amateur athlete. Feist liked Adams and offered him a job as a warehouse clerk for $125 a month—a big salary at the time.

Boots took the job. His plan was to earn enough to pay for his senior year at the University of Kansas, but he never returned to school. He gave his heart and soul to his new employer.

Boots Adams was full of ideas, and in 1921, not long after joining the company, he convinced Phillips executives to sponsor a basketball team as a promotional tool. The Phillips 66ers was a magnificent squad that would win six Amateur Athletic Union national titles and, at the time, was generally considered one of the world's best basketball teams. All the players, including Boots Adams and Bill Feist, worked full time for the company and practiced in their off hours.

Many players from that original team went on to high positions in the company, but no one rose higher and faster than Boots Adams. His meteoric climb through the ranks at Phillips is without parallel in the history of American business. In his first six years with the company, he was promoted from warehouse clerk to assistant to the operations manager of production, then to assistant chief clerk of accounting. In 1927, he was named assistant secretary of the company. One year later, he was assistant treasurer.

In 1932, Frank Phillips, founder of the company, chose Boots to fill the newly created position of assistant to the president. The decision was tantamount to a coronation. By the age of thirty-five, Boots was the company treasurer, a member of the board of directors, and a member of the executive committee.

Boots Adams was one of the most dynamic figures in the history of American business. His personality sucked you in whether you wanted to go or not. He was often overbearing, and he had no fear. He had "the guts of an army mule." On January 1, 1938, he was a company vice-president. Four months later, at the age of thirty-eight, he was the youngest president of a major corporation in America.

Boots Adams and Cloyce Box were very close, probably because they were so much alike. Both men used their powerful and aggressive personalities to get what they wanted. Boots was a frustrated jock who loved sports, and he liked to associate with athletes, like Box. The two men hit it off from the get-go.

"Cloyce met my father in the early '60s," said Gary Adams. "Cloyce was working for George A. Fuller and wanted to buy a cement plant in Pryor, Oklahoma. Someone told Cloyce that if he wanted to start a business in Oklahoma, he needed to see Boots Adams. Cloyce called my father and met him in his office. They connected."[5]

But their bond was more than business and deeper than friendship. Boots was a tower of strength and everything Box thought a man was supposed to be. Box's own father was a fragile man. Boots was the powerhouse father figure Box never really had.

"Boots Adams liked my father," Tom Box recalled. "He took my father under his wing. And Boots was an amazing character. He loved basketball, and my dad was a basketball player. Their relationship began with sports, but it went much farther than that. My father had a great intellectual curiosity, and he sought out interesting people. Boots was an interesting guy. They moved in the same social circles. It was only natural that they became friends."[6]

When Box needed money to buy cement plants and oil refineries, Boots pulled the strings and arranged the loans. The two men were close. Scarcely a day went by for eighteen years that they didn't talk on the phone.

And it wasn't all business. In addition to a deep friendship, the two men shared a sophomoric sense of humor and a taste for practical jokes. Once when Boots had abdominal surgery, he arranged for someone in the operating room to take a picture of his intestines. As a joke, he sent a copy of the picture to Box, but Box went one better.

"Cloyce enlarged it, framed it, and hung it on the wall in his office—by the bathroom," David Ownby, Box's employee recalled. "It was a huge color picture, maybe three feet by four feet, of Boots' intestines hanging out."[7]

That picture, the subject of small talk at the urinal, was an image that symbolized an attribute both men possessed in large quantities.

The relationship between Cloyce Box and Trammell Crow began with an introduction by Doak Walker. Doak was a huge celebrity who knew everyone who was anyone in Dallas.

The relationship strengthened when Box, as district manager of the Dallas office for Fuller Construction Company, built the fourteen-story Bank of New Mexico building in Albuquerque in 1959. Crow owned one-third of the building and was on his way to becoming a very wealthy real estate tycoon with one of the most valuable property portfolios in America.

Although Box was from the country and Crow was a city boy, their backgrounds were similar. They were poor boys who made good. The two men took an instant liking to each other, and their amazing friendship endured almost until the end of their lives.

The attraction of two dynamic personalities and two brilliant minds formed the basis of that friendship.

Trammell Crow was raised, along with his seven brothers and sisters, in a three-room rent house at 1318 Fitzhugh Street in East Dallas.[8] Crow, like Box, had a strong mother and a fragile father. While attending Woodrow Wilson High School, Crow plucked chickens, cleaned bricks, and unloaded boxcars to make money. With his earnings, he paid his way through Southern Methodist University and became the youngest certified public accountant in Texas at the age of twenty-four.

His career began as a teller at the Mercantile National Bank in downtown Dallas—the building with the flying red horse on the roof. When Dallas started to grow after the war, Crow started buying real estate and building warehouses. It all began in the late 1940s with some property on the banks of the Trinity River Crow bought from John Stemmons. Crow built a single-story warehouse on the property and rented it to the Ray-O-Vac Company.

Crow was a groundbreaking entrepreneur who took the commercial real estate business in a bold new direction. In the old days, developers, schooled by the Depression, were cautious. They first found tenants and then built warehouses to meet those tenants' specific demands. But Crow was a speculator. He built warehouses and office buildings first, and then found tenants, using talented and aggressive young salesmen to secure leases.

Crow was a generous man. Many of his young guns, like his protégé Mack Pogue, made fortunes.

Crow was a man of great enthusiasm, charm, and charisma. He was sophisticated but folksy. He was rich as hell, but had a common touch. He believed in openness and trust. He conducted a lot of business with a handshake and without a contract. Bankers, clients, and competitors knew him as a man of honesty and integrity. He was a master dealmaker, but he never went for the last dollar. He always let his counterpart walk away feeling he had made a good deal.

And yet he was tough as a wild hog, and by the mid-1950s Crow was the largest warehouse builder in Dallas. By 1979, he was worth between $50 and $75 million. At his peak, he had an interest in 300 million square feet of warehouse space around the world.

His holdings dwarfed Donald Trump's. The *Wall Street Journal* called him the largest landlord in the United States.

Cloyce Box admired his friend's boundless energy and incredible command of detail. "Exxon would take a hundred professional people to plan its building in New York," Cloyce Box once said. "Trammell Crow would do the whole thing by himself."[9]

Crow built the Trade Mart in Dallas—at the time, the world's largest wholesale merchandise mart. In the early afternoon on November 22, 1963, he waited there for the motorcade bringing President John F. Kennedy for lunch. Instead, the motorcade sped on past to the emergency room at Parkland Hospital. Minutes later, Erik Jonasson, president of the Dallas Citizens Council and future mayor, stepped to the podium and made the shocking announcement that President Kennedy and Governor Connally had been shot as their motorcade moved down Commerce Street.

"My father and Trammell Crow had a special relationship," Tom Box explained. "Trammell was an accountant, but he was much more than that. He was brilliant. He was a builder and an artist with a love for architectural design. My father had the mind of an engineer who could make Trammell's designs a reality. They were naturally drawn to one another."[10]

The two men tossed money around like insincere compliments. Maurice Campbell recalled that "Cloyce Box and Trammell Crow were great friends until they had a falling out over the Midlothian Cement Plant, and what was remarkable about their relationship was how loose they were with their money. They would borrow large amounts of money from each other—millions of dollars—and never sign a thing. Only a verbal agreement to pay it back."[11]

Crow mentored the business careers of Cloyce Box and Roger Staubach. Staubach called Crow, "My Tom Landry Off the Field."

Late in life, Crow developed Alzheimer's. He died in his sleep at his ranch near Tyler on January 14, 2009. At the time of his death, he was worth $7.2 billion, give or take a few million.

Box knew the value of good connections. He served on the advisory board of the Dallas Tornadoes, a professional soccer team owned by his friend Lamar Hunt of the Hunt Oil family—owner of the Kansas City Chiefs and one of the founders of the American Football League. Box served on the board with, among others,

Tom Vandergriff (one of the men who brought the Texas Rangers baseball team to Arlington), flamboyant Dallas mega-car salesman W. O. Bankston (where Box bought his white Lincolns), and Box's old teammate from the Lions, Yale Lary of Hurst.[12]

Box sometimes had dinner at the Mansion on Turtle Creek with Norman and Kelly Green—transplanted Canadians and owners of the Dallas Stars of the National Hockey League. Frank Gifford introduced Box to the Greens. When the Stars first came to Dallas, Box bought season tickets and persuaded his friends to do the same. It was an act of kindness the Greens never forgot.

And Box was an amazing dinner guest. His favorite topic of conversation was cutting horses and thoroughbreds, but he also had an informed fascination with exotic Ecuadorian beetles and Colombian butterflies he learned about on business trips to South America.[13]

Box first met George Herbert Walker Bush at the Martini Bowl on April 29, 1951. The Martini Bowl was a crazy pick-up football game between the Midland Misfits and the Lubbock Leftovers. The Midland players were a collection of ambitious young men out to learn the oil business during the West Texas boom.

"There had been an article in *Life Magazine*," said Bill Liedtke who played for Midland that day. "The area was getting a lot of national publicity, drawing people in from all over. It was a well-educated group that at the same time was pretty down to earth. They were not living off the old man; they were out there to make it on their own, though it didn't hurt to have a few connections through your folks. A lot of us used to play touch football on Sundays behind the high school. Our wives would come down with the kids to watch the amateur athletes run up and down the field until we were exhausted, and then we'd repair to someone's home and have a few beers."[14]

Bill Wiggins, a Dallas oilman who lived in Lubbock at the time, heard about the touch football played by the young Midland oil men and challenged them to a game. The challenge was accepted. The Martini Bowl was set. The Lubbock contingent chartered a bus, loaded it with wives and beer and headed south for Midland.

The Midland Misfits were just a bunch of weekend warriors; guys like Bill Liedtke, Toby Hilliard, John Ashmun, Bill Bovaird, and Liedke's neighbor from across the street, a tall fellow with pretty good hands named George Herbert Walker Bush. At the time, the future president worked for Dresser Industries. Bush's father, Senator Prescott Bush, sat on Dresser's board of directors. The Misfits could hold their own with amateurs, but what the unsuspecting Misfits didn't know was that Bill Wiggins had stacked the deck.

The Lubbock Leftovers were loaded with future Hall of Famer Bobby Layne at quarterback, Malcolm Kutner—an All-American end at the University of Texas, Heisman Trophy winner and All-American running back from Army Glen Davis, Len "Tuffy" McCormick of the Baltimore Colts, and Cloyce Box of the Detroit Lions. The only ringer on the Midland side was Paul Campbell, imported from Odessa—the man who succeeded Bobby Layne at quarterback at the University of Texas.

But the guys from Midland, schooled in the rough and tumble world of the oil business, had a few advantages of their own. The Leftovers drank too much beer on the way down from Lubbock. Glen Davis was distracted by the presence of his new wife, actress Terry Moore (she played the flirty Betty Anderson in the movie *Peyton Place*).

The game was played by Midland rules, which the Misfits made up as they went along. One of the rules that really hurt was that the Leftovers were not allowed to cuss. The referee was John Overbey, George Bush's partner in the oil business.

The game ended in a tie. Overbey, who doubled as the timekeeper, declared that time had expired just as the Leftovers were about to score the winning touchdown. After the game, the teams headed for Bill Bovaird's house for barbecue and more beer.

"Almost all the guys who were in the game out there at that time went on to do fairly well," Leidtke said.

Bill Bovaird started Bovaird Supply—an oil field service company. John Ashmun became CEO of Wainoco Oil. Toby Hilliard started his own oil company. Bill Liedtke, John Overbey, and George Bush, with a loan from the Bush family, would form Zapata Petroleum and Zapata Offshore Drilling. Eventually, the three men would go their separate ways with Liedtke taking Zapata Petroleum, which eventually evolved into Pennzoil. Liedtke would serve as finance chairman for Richard Nixon's presidential campaigns in 1968 and 1972 and for the Bush-Quayle campaign in 1988. Overbey started his own company, and George Bush ran Zapata Offshore until 1966, and then went into politics.[15]

Layne, Davis, McCormick, and Box headed back to the National Football League. That fall, Glenn Davis and the Los Angeles Rams won the NFL Championship. One year later a hit by Hardy Brown of the San Francisco 49ers destroyed his knee and ended his career. Tuffy McCormick graduated from Baylor Law School. Bobby Layne and the Detroit Lions would win three NFL championships in the 1950s. Malcolm Kutner went into the oil business.

But no one on the Lubbock side made out better than Cloyce Box.

On that warm day in West Texas, he established lasting relationships with guys who would become some of the most powerful businessmen and politicians in America, including a future president of the United States.

"My father dealt with extraordinary people all of his life," son Tom recalled. "He never had an ordinary day."[16]

In 1963, Box and a group of businessmen bought Rawlings Sporting Goods Company for $10.5 million. Other investors included John L. Burns—former president of RCA, Frank C. Pace Jr.—former Secretary of the Army and former chairman of General Dynamics, and William A. Shea—a New York attorney best known as the man who led the successful campaign to bring national league baseball back to New York. The city honored Shea by naming the new stadium in Queens after him.[17]

In 1967, Box and his partners bought the Houston franchise of the American Basketball Association for $30 million, hired Hall of Famer Slater Martin as head coach and general manager, tried to lure Wilt Chamberlain to Houston, and then sold the franchise to a group that included Bud Adams, owner of the Houston Oilers and Boots Adams's son.[18]

On October 6, 1969, Governor Preston Smith named nine new members to the West Texas State University Board of Regents. Two of them would earn fame in the business world: Cloyce Box and T. Boone Pickens Jr. Pickens was chairman of Mesa Petroleum and a future billionaire.

For Box, the appointment was a way of repaying his alma mater for all it did for him. The University had changed his life, and he was truly grateful for it.

"It's been a one-way street up to now," he once said. "Everything was free to me—the room, the board, the tuition, books, the fine, solid education. I never really contributed anything commensurate with what I received. I am here because I want to do something now. It is the least I can do."[19]

But Box and Pickens could not get along. Their personalities clashed. Even the vast expanse of West Texas wasn't big enough for the titanic egos of Cloyce Box and Boone Pickens.

When the regents chose Box as chairman, Pickens resigned in protest.[20]

11

Bring Down the Thunder

A man with money is no match against
a man on a mission.

—Doyle Brunson, a.k.a. "Texas Dolly"

In the spring of 1954, Jerry Sullivan, a sports fan and vice president of the George A. Fuller Construction Company of New York City, offered Cloyce Box a full-time job as a design engineer at the new Fuller office in Dallas. Box, who was about to retire from the National Football League, took the job. He was familiar with Fuller having worked part time in the company's legal department processing insurance claims since 1952. Doak Walker joined the company the following year.

The George A. Fuller Construction Company, founded in 1882, was the largest construction company in the world. Fuller was one of the first true general contractors, completing projects by coordinating the work of dozens of subcontractors.

Fuller specialized in skyscrapers. In fact, Fuller built the very first skyscraper: the Flatiron Building at Broadway and 23rd in New York City. Fuller also built some of the most recognizable buildings in the United States including the elegant Plaza Hotel in New York, the United Nations Building, Rockefeller Center, Lincoln Center, and the Lincoln Memorial in Washington, DC. Fuller was the contractor for Penn Station; the Phillips Petroleum Building in Bartlesville, Oklahoma; and the Louisiana State Capitol in Baton Rouge. On a much smaller scale, Fuller developed the Quonset hut—a prefabricated all-purpose metal building that could be shipped anywhere and assembled with unskilled labor.

Box may have got the job at Fuller because he was a famous jock, but anyone who doubted his business skills and flaming ambition got a rude awakening. He had no plans to sit quietly and draw his pay. His aim was to climb the corporate ladder all the way to the top, and he focused his tremendous energy to that purpose. He learned quickly and impressed everyone with his work ethic, intelligence, and dynamic personality.

One person who took notice was Louis Crandall, Fuller's CEO.

Louis Crandall was another rich and powerful man who was smitten by Box, and Crandall was a man not easily impressed. He had seen it all. Lou Crandall, like Boots Adams, Oscar Wyatt, Trammell Crow, and Cloyce Box, had ambition to burn and a supercharged personality. As a young man, Crandall worked at Fuller as a junior executive. Then in 1928, at the tender age of thirty-four, he became the CEO of the largest construction company on the planet.

Crandall met Box soon after Box went to work at the Fuller office in Dallas. Promotions and pay raises swiftly followed. In 1955, Box began working directly with Fred M. Kaiser, the head of the Dallas office. Five years later, Crandall promoted Box to office manager. By 1962, he was regional vice president of the company and sat on its board of directors with a salary that was the envy of any professional athlete.

Box's personality was larger than life, but he was not all style and flash. Lou Crandall could see that Box had a flair for administration and the rare combination of knowledge, interpersonal skills, and instincts required to run a large company. Educated in business, engineering, and law, Box had superb academic credentials. But more than that, he had an unusual ability to track and coordinate the work of hundreds of workers and dozens of subcontractors on multiple projects. He worked long hours and was meticulous in his preparation. He was laser focused with an unusual ability to tune out distractions. He was a perfectionist and super attentive to detail.

Box was also an ex-marine who commanded respect and attention. He knew how to handle his employees. The "Box treatment" was a combination of physical intimidation, flattery, and coercion. He could be warm and personal or blunt and direct. He could put on the charm or bring down the thunder, whatever was necessary to get the job done. His "no" was as final as a slamming door. Box could give an order in Dallas and make it happen halfway around the world. Not an easy thing to do.

In December 1964, Cloyce, Fern, and the boys (Don, Gary, Tom, and Doug) were in Los Angeles for the holidays. It was a rare time away from work for Box. Perhaps some family time in LA might brighten holiday spirits. But before he could get into the rhythm of the season, a phone call changed everything.

The call was from Lou Crandall in New York. Crandall had just turned seventy-one and was ready to hand over company leadership to Fuller's two brightest stars: Bill Lawson, a senior vice president who happened to be Crandall's son-in-law, and Cloyce Box.

"Come to New York and run the company," Crandall said to Box.

Box wanted to run the company—that had been his desire all along, but he did not want to live and work in New York. He liked Texas and had reasons for staying put. By 1964, he had extensive commercial interest in the Southwest. In addition to his job as regional vice president at Fuller, he was running a cement company in Oklahoma and another in Louisiana. He had just bought a 300-acre ranch near Dallas.

Ever since Cloyce was a boy in Jonesboro, his dream was to be a Texas country gentleman. He wanted to live in a big fancy house on a hill. He wanted to raise cattle and horses. He wanted to be a Texas big shot. He wanted to drive around Dallas in his Lincoln Continental talking on his car phone and singing, "Make the World Go Away" with the Tennessee Plowboy.

In Texas, he stood out from the crowd. In New York, he was just another tall Texan with money. Most New Yorkers didn't even own cars. They used public transportation. What kind of a life was that? Box thought New Yorkers were crazy.

He was equally uninterested in the proposed working arrangement at Fuller. He had no desire to share the responsibility of running Fuller with Bill Lawson or anyone else. Besides, Box and Lawson had very different approaches to the construction business. Lawson wanted to keep Fuller on the same conservative course the company had followed since the 1880s, while Box favored a new direction for Fuller and a more aggressive Trammell Crow-like approach to the construction business.

And Box despised the idea of shared leadership. He was supremely confident in his abilities with an overwhelming desire to be in control. In his organization, there would be no shared decision making or administration by committee. The man at the top would call the shots.

"Fire me, but I'll not move to New York for a damn job," Box bluntly told Crandall.

Then Box dropped the bombshell. "But if you want out I'll buy you out."[1]

There were no details, but Crandall knew the offer was serious. Box was never flippant about business.

Crandall's response was equally serious. He would sell his Fuller shares to Box, if Box could arrange financing, but only if Box would buy out all the major stockholders and if Bill Lawson was a part of the ownership group. Lou Crandall drove a hard bargain.

Box caught the next plane back to Dallas to think it over. Fern and the boys stayed in Los Angeles. Family togetherness would have to wait for another time.

On reflection, he decided to accept Crandall's offer but with a complicated caveat that was vintage Cloyce Box. He wanted to buy a majority of Fuller stock, take it off the American Stock Exchange, and make it a private company.

The arrangement had advantages: no stockholders to answer to, fewer government regulations, less red tape, and fewer hassles.

The idea of making Fuller a private company probably came from Box's recent experience as a part of the ownership group at Rawlings Sporting Goods Company—at the time the only privately owned sporting goods manufacturer in the United States.

Of course, turning a large publically owned organization like Fuller into a private company would be one of the most complex business transactions ever attempted, but Box was certain it could be done. He would need money and he would need help from friends in high places.

The next day he paid a visit to Trammell Crow.

Crow balked, at first. He made his fortune in warehouses and commercial real estate and had purposely stayed away from the construction business. But Crow had faith in his friend, and by the end of meeting, Crow had changed his mind. Even legends had a hard time saying no to Cloyce Box.

With Trammell Crow on board, Box went to work building the complex partnerships the deal required. The purchasing group Box put together included himself, Trammell Crow, Bill Lawson, and Maurice Moore, Crow's friend and the head of a company called Western Sales Ltd.—a Bahamian corporation with Transcontinental Bus System Inc. as the majority stockholder. Moore, from Jackson, Tennessee, could hold his own in Box's circle of fast friends. He began his career as an 18-year-old ticket agent at the bus station in Little Rock, Arkansas, and by tenacity and brute force rose all the way to the top.[2]

Together, the four investors formed BCLM Inc., a Maryland corporation that took its name from the first letter of the last name of the four men who formed it.[3] At one point, David and Winthrop Rockefeller showed an interest in joining the group (Trammell Crow and Cloyce Box met Winthrop Rockefeller, the Governor of Arkansas, through Maurice Moore), but after some consideration the brothers pronounced the transaction "too complicated" and withdrew.[4] (Although this deal with the Rockefellers fell through, Box made another powerful connection. Soon he and the Rockefellers would do one of the biggest real estate deals of all time.)

But this was clearly Box's deal. He was the point man, and he was superb. He made all the arrangements and took care of all the details.

His plan was for BCLM to take over Fuller, its name, and its assets for $16 million. One of the interesting parts of the plan was that each of the four partners put up only $250,000. They borrowed the remaining $15 million, using the company itself as collateral, in what is known as a leveraged buyout. (Box probably got the idea from the car business. When he sold a Buick, the bank financed the purchase using the car as collateral. Box just used the same arrangement, on a much larger scale.)

"The Fuller deal was one of the first leveraged buyouts ever done," Tom Box explained. "A leveraged buyout is a deal where the assets of the company being acquired are used as collateral to meet the cost of acquisition. It is a technique that allows buyers to make large acquisitions without having to commit large amounts of cash. Leveraged buyouts are fairly common today, but my father and Trammell Crow were among the first. It was a huge deal at the time. Maybe $2 billion in today's dollars."[5]

The purchase package included sizeable loans from Lloyd's of London, New York Life Insurance Company, and David Rockefeller's Chase Manhattan Bank.[6] Box proposed that BCLM use its loans to pay $37 a share for Fuller stock currently selling at 34.75 on the American Stock Exchange.

But it was the part of the plan that returned Fuller, a public corporation since the 1920s, to a privately held company that caught Wall Street and the business world by surprise.

The Fuller board of directors, dominated by Crandall, Box, and Lawson, quickly approved the BCLM's nonnegotiable offer with little discussion in April 1965, declaring in a proxy statement to shareholders that the $37 per share offer was fair in light of the company's recent history and prospects in the very competitive general contracting field. Company profits in 1964 were down over a million dollars from the previous year, and predictions for the coming year were no better.

Still, some shareholders did not like the proposal, claiming that insiders would end up getting the company at a bargain price. Some shareholders accused Lou Crandall of orchestrating the buyout in order to turn Fuller over to his son-in-law.[7]

The proposal came to a vote on June 7, 1965, at a special meeting of Fuller stockholders in a small law office at 117 Main Street in Flemington, New Jersey, twenty miles north of Trenton. The building was made of faded clapboard, built in the mid-1800s, with a history that appealed to Cloyce Box's sense of destiny. Republic Steel, United Fruit, and Eastman Kodak, among many other large corporations, had been chartered in that old building. Now Fuller Construction Company and Cloyce Box would make business history there.[8]

The meeting was tense, "almost three hours of shirtsleeved wrangling," exacerbated by the cramped quarters and unusually high summer temperatures in a building with no air-conditioning.[9] Opponents of the sale claimed that the remote location, the small meeting space, and the disagreeable conditions were a strategy to discourage angry stockholders from attending the meeting and voting against the deal.

At that meeting, one group of shareholders fought to keep the company public. The group protested BCLM's tactics as heavy-handed and questioned the nomination of the vote inspectors, believing the inspectors to be biased in favor of the proposed buyers.

But company officers ran the meeting, and they rammed the proposal through despite the protests. Chairman Crandall listened quietly and calmly to the objections and complaints. Even when the rhetoric was heated, he never lost his cool.

Then when the sweaty participants seemed to be talked out, Crandall rose from his chair, threw back his shoulders, and sternly announced that of the 429,344 outstanding shares of common stock, 303,245 (70%) voted, most by proxy, in favor of the proposal.[10] (The deal needed a two-thirds vote for approval.) With that announcement, he banged the gavel and Fuller became the largest company in history to revert from public to private ownership.[11]

The closing took place two days later and was vintage Cloyce Box—overstated and complex. He left nothing to chance. No detail was overlooked. Every movement was choreographed. Even Trammell Crow, no slouch when it came to details, was impressed.

"The closing," as Crow remembered, "was attended by at least a hundred different lawyers and principals. It was so complicated that the closing had its own Master and required a three-hour rehearsal on closing eve and ten hours to execute on closing day."[12]

With the closing complete, Cloyce Box owned 25 percent of the company and, after reorganization, became Fuller's CEO. Within weeks, he delisted the stock and moved the corporate headquarters from its office in New York to a steel and glass office tower overlooking Stemmons Freeway just north of downtown Dallas.

Box hit the ground running and immediately launched Fuller on a building frenzy. The company built the $45.7 million Metropolitan Opera House in New York and the forty-five-story Plaza Towers in New Orleans. Fuller did the advance design and engineering work on the Superconducting Super Collider—a massive particle accelerator to be built under 16,000 acres of prairie land near Waxahachie, Texas. Scientists thought the project was necessary to continue the study of high-energy physics, but taxpayers cringed at the cost (somewhere between $4 and $12 billion). Congress eventually defunded it.

In 1967, Fuller broke ground on Embarcadero Center in downtown San Francisco. At the time it was built, Embarcadero Center, called Rockefeller Center West, was one of the largest privately owned business and entertainment centers in the world. The complex contained three office towers, an 800-room convention hotel, three theaters, shops, restaurants, art galleries, and underground parking for 2,000 cars. The entire complex contained 2.85 million square feet of commercial office space. The tallest office building was sixty stories, making it the tallest structure in the city, surpassing the fifty-three-story Bank of America building. The price tag for the project was $125,000,000.

David Rockefeller, president of Chase Manhattan Bank of New York, and Winthrop Rockefeller, the Governor of Arkansas, owned 50 percent of the completed project. The other 50 percent was split among architect John Portman from Atlanta, Cloyce Box, and Trammell Crow.[13] (In 2013, Embarcadero Center sold to Boston Properties for $1.2 billion.) Each of the owners contributed something to the project. Portman designed it, Box built it, Crow leased it, and the Rockefellers supplied prestige and money.

Fuller seemed to be flying high under Box's watch, but there were difficulties at the company that were slow to surface in a privately owned corporation whose books were closed to public view. Fuller was struggling financially, even as it built concrete monuments at a furious pace.

One problem was the culture shock brought on by the move of company headquarters from New York to Texas. Fuller had an eastern culture and most of its business was in that part of the country. Many of Fuller's eastern clients had trouble dealing with the crazy Texans from Dallas. The things that mattered most to Cloyce Box were an enigma to New Yorkers. Easterners had no appreciation for cattle or horses and didn't care a lick for country music.

Of course, the troubles at Fuller were more serious than diverse styles and different accents. "By the time dad left the company, Fuller was overextended," Doug Box explained. "My father was an aggressive guy. While he was president the company took on too many projects and too much debt." By the summer of 1969, Fuller Construction Company had over $1 billion in projects underway around the world.[14]

With rising costs of labor and materials and declining profits, Cloyce Box and Trammell Crow decided to sell their shares of Fuller, but found no takers at the asking price. Even a casual glance at company records revealed several areas of concern. Fuller had $200 to $300 million worth of performance bonds outstanding, and creditors were worried. (A performance bond is a promise issued by an insurance company or a bank to guarantee satisfactory completion of a project by a contractor.)

Then personalities and egos, placated when profits were up, clashed when profits went down. After a Dallas Skyline High School project turned into a fiasco, the ownership group that Box had so carefully assembled was no longer a big happy family. Box and Crow fell out with Lou Crandall and Bill Lawson. Maurice Moore was not satisfied with his share of the profits.

Trammell Crow, who had arranged for much of the private capital, was worried. He faced "a risk that could have been more than I could handle." But the "Box treatment" saved the day. Box negotiated a sale of Fuller Construction to Northrup Aviation in which he and Crow broke even. In the end, Box "brought him (Crow) back alive."[15]

Although Box's tenure at Fuller was a disappointment, the experience was invaluable.

"Dad learned a lot at Fuller that would serve him well later on," Doug Box explained. "He overextended the company, but out of that experience, he learned how to build refineries, and he learned how to build cement plants. Fuller ended on a sour note, but the experience was the genesis for the rest of his business career."[16]

Box's tenure at Fuller was a sobering experience, and from it, he learned hard lessons that changed forever the way he did business. At Fuller, he was not always among friends. Going forward, he would surround himself only with people he knew and trusted. He became obsessive about secrecy and he learned to protect himself. In future deals, he would go to extraordinary lengths to shield his personal investment, even if he had to stretch the rules to the breaking point.

Box saw opportunities to make money all around him, and it was while he looked down from the Fuller office at 1949 Stemmons Freeway in Dallas that he was first drawn to the cement business. Many of the people stuck in rush-hour traffic outside Box's window worked in Dallas but lived on prairie land that a short time ago was cotton fields and cow pastures near the once small towns of Garland, Irving, Grand Prairie, Plano, Carrollton, and Mesquite. The endless line of cars crawling by was proof that the American geographic and economic landscape was changing. Americans were leaving the automobile assembly lines and rusty steel mills in the Northeast and the Midwest for jobs in aerospace, oil, and defense—industries concentrated in the southwest.

Even within the state and region, people were moving from rural areas to the cities in unprecedented numbers. Starving farmers, unable to make a living on a few hundred acres, were selling out (or in some cases walking away) and moving to the city to work in the factories with 40-hour weeks, fixed wages, and company benefits. Houston, Dallas, Fort Worth, Oklahoma City, and Tulsa were busting at the seams.

The great southwest building boom was on. Cloyce Box could see the evidence in the freeways, bridges, and buildings outside his window. Some people saw an interesting trend, but he saw dollar signs.

If America were to become a concrete jungle, Box would provide the cement.

The CEO of Fuller Construction Company was a busy man. He worked late hours and weekends, and he was always closing the next deal. His work was his life. His family didn't see him for days at a time.

Box was a member of at least three Dallas-area country clubs (Preston Trail, Bent Tree, and Brook Hollow), but rarely played a round of golf at any of them. He never wasted his time on things that were of no interest to him.

While other men had a passion for hunting, fishing, or golf, Box loved to fly. He learned to fly in Korea, and like Icarus, he was exhilarated by flight. He loved flying so much that he sometimes flew when driving was more convenient. His sister Wilmuth claimed, "he used planes like the rest of us use cars."[17]

He liked to travel high, fast, and in style, and in 1967 he traded in his Aero Commander for a Learjet. With two corporate offices in different cities (Dallas and Tulsa) and projects underway all over the country, he needed fast, reliable transportation.

He was an excellent pilot although his methods were unorthodox. He rarely filed a flight plan. In aviation as in everything else in his life, Box never doubted his own judgment.

One day, an air traffic controller had the scare of his life when a seven-passenger Learjet came in low over the horizon and touched down on the fearfully short runway in Ruston, Louisiana. Box was in town to talk business with the T. L. James Company and to pay a social call to Joe Aillet, his old football coach at Louisiana Tech, and no technicality, like a short runway, could keep him from doing what he wanted.[18]

On weekends, Box often flew from his home in Frisco to the Box Ranch near Waco. "My ranch was right next to his out between Moody and Spring Valley," his friend and neighbor Maurice Campbell said. "We are both from Jonesboro, and we knew each other. I did some legal work for him, and we became friends. I think I was a connection to his past, and we had a special relationship. He needed that connection with his childhood. It was important to him."

"I remember a time when every Saturday I would cook a big meal of pinto beans, cornbread, and boiled onions. Then about noon, just like clockwork, a plane would buzz my house. It was Cloyce flying in from Frisco."

"That sound was my signal to get in my truck and pick Cloyce up at his place. He had a landing strip just down the hill from his house on Box Ranch Road. It's a funny thing, but he could have had lunch at any of the finest restaurants in New York or Dallas, but he loved to come to my house every Saturday for pinto beans, cornbread, and boiled onions. It reminded him of his mother and his childhood. For a little while he was back in Jonesboro."[19]

"He flew from Dallas to the Box Ranch in a Beechcraft King Air," Doug Box recalled. "The experts told him not to land it in a field, but dad didn't listen to the experts. He did what he wanted."[20]

Frank Gifford never forgot the first time he and Box went airborne. "In the 1960s I was working for ABC's Wide World of Sports*," Gifford explained. "I remember going to Dallas to do a piece on Cloyce. It was one of those 'where are they now' pieces. Well, after we had finished, I needed to go to Oklahoma City, and Cloyce offered to fly me there in one of his jets. We were up there flying along over North Texas. Cloyce was in the pilot's seat, and I was sitting in the co-pilot's seat. The plane was on automatic pilot. I was lost in thought. Cloyce hadn't said anything for a while, and when I looked at him, he was asleep. Scared the hell out of me."*[21]

David Ownby once flew with Box from Addison to Purcell, Oklahoma. It was a trip Ownby would never forget.

"He was a very unconventional pilot," Ownby said with a laugh. "As soon as we took off, Cloyce hands me a road atlas. 'What's this for?' I said, and he said, 'we're following I-35 to Purcell. You're my navigator.' He didn't file a flight plan so I guess the only way to find Purcell, Oklahoma was to follow the highway."

"I'm glad it wasn't cloudy. Not sure where we would have ended up."[22]

Doug Box remembered the time he and his father "flew to Ruidoso, New Mexico, to see a horse race. The flight was uneventful until dad radioed the tower that we were coming in, but the landing gear wouldn't go down. I was nervous, but dad was mad as hell. He finally cranked the landing gear down by hand, but even in that dangerous moment my father wasn't fearful. He was angry. He wasn't afraid of anything."[23]

12

Written in Concrete

High achievers spot rich opportunities swiftly, make big decisions quickly and move into action immediately.

—Robert Schuller

Cement is made by heating limestone (calcium carbonate) with small quantities of clay and shale, in a kiln. The heating process makes a substance called *clinker* that is then ground with gypsum into a fine powder to make Portland cement. Dry cement is then mixed with water and an aggregate (usually sand, gravel, or crushed stone) to make a remarkable substance called *concrete*—a material that is indispensable to the modern construction industry.

There was a time when the demand for cement was soft. Concrete, particularly in large amounts, can be tricky to work with, and before the 1950s, the high cost of mixing and transporting heavy concrete was prohibitive. Consequently, its use only made sense on very large projects, like river dams, where it was mixed on-site. Then in the 1950s, the cement/concrete business went through a transformation that made concrete more functional and the cement business far more profitable. Cloyce Box saw the trend and capitalized on it.

The high demand for concrete arose because of the 1950s building boom fed by the proliferation of ready-mix concrete plants. Ready-mix plants solved a big problem for contractors. Ready-mix plants mixed concrete in large batches according to a set recipe and transported it to the construction site in large trucks.

Before ready-mix plants, concrete was not user-friendly. After ready-mix plants, builders found all kinds of uses for concrete.

Contractors used reinforced concrete, mixed at ready-mix plants and transported in special trucks, for highways, bridges, commercial buildings, and for the foundations of the millions of new homes being built every year. Earlier homes had pier and beam foundations made of wood.

There are some downsides to the cement business. Cement plants are complex and incredibly expensive. The high construction costs tend to keep competition to a minimum, but the lack of competition leads to fears of price-fixing and causes government officials to pay close attention to cement prices. The production process can also be dirty, and the smokestack emissions invite the wrath of environmentalists and the scrutiny of government regulators.

Still, a cement plant, optimally located and in the hands of a skilled businessman, can be a gold mine.

In the early 1950s a group of Oklahoma businessmen, primarily in the rock quarrying business, discovered a natural geological formation containing alternating layers of shale and limestone (the ingredients for cement), thirty miles east of Tulsa, near the town of Pryor, Oklahoma. The men founded the Ozark Cement Company and built a small cement plant near the formation. (Because the cost of transporting the heavy raw materials for making cement is prohibitive, cement plants are typically located at the quarry site.) But the Oklahoma businessmen were inexperienced with the cement business and soon went bankrupt.

Cloyce Box learned of the bankrupt cement plant in 1958. He was in the construction business, and from his position at Fuller, he knew that demand for cement was on the rise in the Tulsa area. He sensed that this was the business opportunity of a lifetime.

Box wanted to buy the plant but needed a million dollars to buy it and renovate it. That's when someone suggested he pay a call to Boots Adams. In addition to being the CEO of Phillips Petroleum, Boots was a director of the First National Bank of Tulsa and was in a position to bankroll Box's project. Box arranged to meet Boots in Tulsa.

The two men made an instant connection. What's more, Boots could smell a good business opportunity. After a 10-minute conversation, Box was in the cement business.[1]

Just as Box was climbing the corporate ladder at Fuller, he organized the Oklahoma Cement Company, later shortened to OKC Corp., with offices in the First National Bank Building in Tulsa. The four founding entities of OKC were the George A. Fuller Company with Cloyce Box acting as regional vice president, Central States Investments with K. S. Adams Sr. as president, Laird and Company of Wilmington, Delaware (distillers) with George T. Weymouth as president, and Coastal States Gas Producing Company with Oscar Wyatt as chairman and president.[2]

The founders and stockholders of the new company showed their confidence in Box by electing him president and chairman of the board, but businessmen talk loudest with their money. Boots Adams would eventually own over 1 million shares of OKC stock. By 1961, Oscar Wyatt's company, Costal States Gas, owned 14.4 percent of OKC's common stock, and Oscar himself sat on OKC's board of directors.[3]

In the process of starting the new company, Boots Adams introduced Box to Robert S. Kerr—oilman, governor, and three-term senator from Oklahoma. Nothing of importance happened in Oklahoma without Kerr's blessing. He was a good man to have on your side if you wanted to sell lots of cement for large government projects.

Box and Kerr quickly became friends.

Meanwhile, the George A. Fuller Company did the engineering and the construction work on the Pryor cement plant beginning in May 1959, and the plant produced its first batch of cement on July 6, 1960.

At the same time, OKC opened a sales office in Tulsa and began marketing cement in the face of stiff competition from three established cement companies in the area. But a talented sales team, aggressive marketing techniques, and friends in the right places paid off. Sales exceeded even bullish expectations, and the company showed a profit its first quarter.[4]

Profits continued to rise, and in October 1961, OKC awarded Fuller a second contract for expansion in order to double the yearly output from 1 to 2 million barrels. Vigorous sales efforts soon had the expanded capacity fully sold. The company built new terminals in Oklahoma City and Woodward.

Demand was brisk, and the timing could not have been better. America was building highways, bridges, and buildings at a furious pace. With Box's connections, OKC supplied the cement to build the Keystone Dam in northeast Oklahoma and the Robert S. Kerr Dam near Pryor, as well as large interstate highway and commercial projects.

Then to raise capital for expansion and diversification, OKC went public. The company became a corporation with stocks bought and sold on the American Stock Exchange and later the New York Stock Exchange. Investors liked the company and its aggressive leadership.

Cloyce Box now had plenty of cash, a proven record as a moneymaker, and a line of credit a mile long, and on December 13, 1962, he announced plans to build a $12 million cement plant with a 1.5-million-barrel capacity on Michoud Canal near the Michoud-Saturn Plant in New Orleans, Louisiana (where the Saturn moon rockets were made).[5] Like the Pryor, Oklahoma, plant, timing and circumstance favored the South Louisiana facility. New Orleans was growing and I-10 was under construction from New Orleans to Baton Rouge.

The first full year of operation, the plant shipped 966,916 barrels of cement with a commercial value of $3.77 million. Most of the cement went to ready-mix plants, oil well servicing companies, and public works projects. The cement produced by the Michoud plant that year amounted to 23 percent of the total shipments of cement in the New Orleans area.

But Box was not satisfied with 23 percent. He was aggressive by nature and wanted to expand his share of the market. So in 1969, he began buying shares in a company called Jahncke Service Inc. of Metairie, Louisiana. Jahncke, in business on the Louisiana Gulf Coast for almost one hundred years, was a subsidiary of Zapata Offshore whose principal owner until 1966 was George H. W. Bush, Box's friend from the early days in the West Texas oil patch.[6]

Jahncke was a diverse company engaged in offshore rig maintenance and support, dredging rivers, dredging and sale of marine shell (used as an aggregate in the manufacture of concrete), and production of ready-mix concrete—which was the part of the business that really interested Cloyce Box.

But there was more to this deal than met the eye. Jahncke was Box's biggest competitor in South Louisiana. OKC already controlled 23 percent of the cement market in South Louisiana, and it was Box's desire to have more that first put him at odds with government regulators.

There are federal laws on the books making it illegal for businesses to buy up similar businesses in order to eliminate competition (and potentially drive up prices). On July 16, 1969, a federal district judge in New Orleans, reacting to complaints and citing a potential decrease in competition in the cement market if OKC acquired control of Jahncke, stepped in and stopped Box from buying more Jahncke stock.[7]

For many businessmen, the story would have ended there, but Box was no ordinary businessman. He and his attorney took on the federal government in court and had the restraining order lifted. He then continued buying shares in Jahncke, eventually assuming control of the company in late 1969. With the acquisition of Jahncke, Box and OKC Corp. had a 5-million-barrel annual capacity between the ready-mix facilities in Pryor, Oklahoma, and New Orleans and controlled the lion's share of the cement market in South Louisiana.

Box won the opening fight with federal regulators, but he made a ton of enemies in Washington. The legal battles between Box and Washington regulators would rage for another quarter century.

Within weeks, an army of agents from the Federal Trade Commission (FTC) were in New Orleans to take a closer look at Cloyce Box's business dealings—particularly the recent acquisition of Jahncke. The FTC is an independent agency of the US Government whose mission is to protect the consumer by insuring competition in the marketplace and preventing anticompetitive business practices—especially coercive monopolies.

After an investigation, an FTC examiner found that Box's acquisition of Jahncke "tended to lessen competition" in the selling of cement in the New Orleans area, and he charged Box with a violation of the Clayton Act and Section 5 of the FTC Act. As a remedy, the examiner ordered Box to sell Jahncke's ready-mix concrete business in order to restore competition in the marketplace.[8]

Box appealed the ruling directly to the FTC in Washington, and after a hearing the FTC handed down its decision—a ruling that did not go in Box's favor. Regulators had serious doubts that Jahncke's ready-mix business would survive "if separated from its parent corporation" and therefore ordered Box to sell not only the ready-mix business but the entire company. The FTC wanted to ensure "a restoration of competition in the cement and ready-mix industries in the New Orleans metropolitan area."[9]

Box had six months to sell Jahncke.[10] He appealed the decision, but the appellate court ruled against him.[11] The lower court ruling stood.

The battle over Jahncke was only the beginning of a long and nasty war between Cloyce Box and the FTC. Box had come from nothing to be a position of wealth and power, and nobody was going to tell him how to run his business, especially some liberal government official who had never created a job and had never made a dime except at the taxpayers' expense.

Box eventually complied with the court order and sold his shares of Jahncke, but with a clever twist that he must have found amusing in light of his well-known contempt for the FTC. Box sold the business to Don Baxter, who just happened to be his close friend and business associate. In fact, Baxter quit his job at OKC Corp. to assume ownership of Jahncke. Not only that, Box loaned Baxter the money to buy Jahncke, and then rehired Baxter as a broker at OKC where Baxter earned the money to repay his loan with interest.[12]

Box's methods weren't always pretty, but they were effective. OKC began with a $1 million loan in 1959. By 1978, the company had assets of $127 million. A thousand-dollar investment in OKC in 1959 would have grown to $33,370 by 1978—an annual return of 22 percent.[13]

13

Sweet Deal

God created mankind upright, but they have gone in search of many schemes.

—Ecclesiastes 7:29

On October 31, 1966, a business called Okmulgee Refining Company, a recently formed and wholly-owned subsidiary of OKC Corp., bought an old Phillips Petroleum oil refinery in Okmulgee, Oklahoma. Cloyce Box made the deal on the advice of Boots Adams and Bill Hulsey, a vice president at Chase Manhattan Bank.

Encouraged by Trammell Crow and Oscar Wyatt and financed with loans arranged by Boots Adams, Box "flipped it," conveniently using his resources at Fuller to turn the old refinery into a state-of-the-art 19,000-barrel-a-day facility, producing various petroleum products including motor fuels, heating oils, jet fuels, diesel fuels, liquefied petroleum gas (LPG), asphalt, asphalt emulsions, and road oils.[1] What's more, in a very cozy business arrangement, Phillips Petroleum supplied all the crude and bought half the output.[2]

The arrangement was a good one for both companies, and for a while, business was brisk. Then all hell broke loose.

First Boots Adams stepped down as chairman of the board of Phillips Petroleum, and when he did, OKC lost its cozy arrangement with the oil giant.

Then the entire oil business went through a chaotic transformation. As domestic production peaked and began to decline, the focus of world energy shifted from the familiar plains of West

Texas to the vast oil fields of the Middle East. There was a great sandstorm ahead for the oil business.

The storm blew in on October 16, 1973. On that day, the Arab members of OPEC (Organization of Petroleum Exporting Countries) decided to punish the United States for backing Israel in the Yom Kippur War. The punishment came in the form of crude oil price hikes and a series of 5 percent reductions in oil production. The decrease in production caused a major disruption of supply channels and an energy crisis the likes of which this world had never seen.

Almost overnight, there was a fourfold increase in the world price of oil and a new set of dynamics in the oil business. The price of gasoline skyrocketed, and there were long lines at the pump. The event was a milestone in the history of twentieth century America. The era of dirt-cheap energy prices had ended.

Refineries, especially small ones, had a hard time finding crude oil at any price. Business turned brutal. The big oil companies used every trick in the book to protect themselves by eliminating competition.

As the crude oil supply tightened, Phillips needed all the crude it could get. The company and its new management wanted out of its preferred arrangement with the Okmulgee Refining Company.

The new leadership at Phillips began putting the squeeze on OKC by raising pipeline fees and jacking up the price of crude oil, it shipped to the Okmulgee refinery. OKC fought back by suing Phillips for breach of contract. The two companies finally reached a settlement with a court order that terminated all supply and sales contracts.

The federal government tried to reduce market volatility and stabilize prices by establishing price controls and by dictating where refineries could sell their products. Simply put, federal regulations mandated that a refinery could only sell to customers it served in 1972, and only when a 1972 customer turned down his allocation could that oil be placed in a pool and reallocated to new customers.

The times ahead would be challenging for the entire industry, but small independent refineries, like Okmulgee, were particularly vulnerable.

Alone in his office at Suite 700 in the George A. Fuller Building at 1949 Stemmons Freeway in Dallas, Cloyce Box pondered his future in the oil business. He searched the laws and federal regulations for wiggle room and loopholes, and he found some. Over the next few weeks, he devised a daring plan to make money refining petroleum in a crazy new world.

In the early months of 1974, six new oil brokers quietly filed applications with the federal government. (A *broker* is a person who arranges transactions between buyers and sellers and takes a commission.) All six were new to the brokering business. All six worked exclusively with OKC Corp. selling unallocated petroleum products.

Most important of all was that each of the six new brokers had a close personal relationship with Cloyce Box. The brokers were, in Box's own words, "people we selected very carefully, a created organization," designed to move the company's refined products on the market.

None of the new brokers had facilities to store or transport petroleum. The "buy and sell transactions were with brokers who had no inventory and no product to actually transfer." They were paper transactions only. In most cases, the ownership of the product changed hands several times but the product never moved from its storage facility at Okmulgee until delivery to the buyer.[3]

The brokers included John R. Adams of Guymon, Oklahoma (no relation to Boots Adams), Box's partner in a quarter-horse farm in Florida; Robert Whitley Sr., Box's old friend from Central Texas; Edwin Gummelt Jr., Robert Whitley's partner in a Waco, Texas oil company; and Cloyce's brother Boyce. One new broker was Cloyce Box's personal secretary who continued to draw her salary from OKC, even as she brokered gasoline and diesel in partnership with her brother. From 1974 to 1979, two-thirds of all OKC sales went through one of these friendly brokers.[4]

As soon as the brokers received government approval, some unusual and controversial business deals began going down.

In November 1975, a company called National Petroleum Sales placed an order with OKC for 22,000 barrels of asphalt. Rather than sell the asphalt directly to the company that placed the order, someone at OKC rerouted the order to John R. Adams. OKC first sold the asphalt to Adams at the regulated price of $8.50 a barrel, and then Adams, free from government price controls, resold the asphalt to National Petroleum Sales for $9.58 a barrel. The broker made over $23,000.

Soon after that, a Farmland Industries subsidiary placed an order with OKC for a large quantity of gasoline. Again, the order was rerouted to one of the new brokers. OKC sold the gasoline to the broker for 35.6 cents a gallon who resold the gasoline to Farmland Industries for 36.5 cents a gallon. On that one transaction, the broker made $84,000.[5]

In another deal, the Department of Energy (DOE) reported that John R. Adams purchased 1.5 million barrels of home heating oil from OKC. Adams immediately resold the oil for more than 150 percent markup, making a profit of $463,900.

Then things got really interesting. Following the money trail, the DOE report claimed that Adams kept $90,284 and paid commissions of $196,826 to each of two men who were partners with Adams and Box in their horseracing business. According to the report, the two men who received the commissions then deposited a total of $225,000 into the account of "Double RR Farms" in an El Paso Bank. Then over the next few weeks, Cloyce Box received five checks on the account for "various racehorse transactions." Those five checks totaled exactly $225,000.[6]

Coincidence? Not so, according to the DOE. They accused Box of circumventing federal regulations by selling petroleum first to friendly brokers at controlled prices who then resold the oil at prices higher than the DOE allowed.[7] Then, according to the DOE, the brokers split their commissions with Box, laundering the money by running it through various bank accounts. The DOE also charged that the practice of selling to the friendly brokers continued even after federal price controls were lifted. (Most of the controls were lifted in 1976 and 1977.)

To be fair, there is nothing unusual about refineries using brokers to sell their products, and it is not illegal for brokers to make handsome commissions. Brokers provide a service to refineries by helping locate customers, eliminating the refinery's need for a large sales force. Brokers were particularly important in the days of the Arab oil embargo. They knew who had goods to sell and who wanted to buy.

Some brokers simply match buyers and sellers and take a commission, while others act as speculators, taking great financial risks by using their own money to buy reserves of gasoline and diesel in hopes of selling those reserves later at a profit. There is nothing wrong or illegal with using a broker. It is a common practice. A legitimate broker earns his commission by providing a valuable service for his client.

But certain government regulators and business media correspondents claimed the arrangement between Cloyce Box and his private brokers was one of the sweetest deals of all time—for the brokers. They made huge profits, and they didn't have to work too hard for their commissions. In fact, the sale was already made before the broker got the call. Some company officials and stockholders wondered if the brokers were any benefit at all to the company.

OKC arranged and orchestrated every transaction. An order would come in, and Cloyce Box would determine which broker would get the order and the selling price. An OKC official would then call the broker, tell him who to contact, and the other details. Occasionally, an OKC official would even close the deal if the broker was especially busy. OKC even made the delivery in its own trucks.

The *New York Times* reported that Box's brokers also received special privileges unavailable to other brokers. For example, there were no penalties for late payment. OKC's credit manager considered payment within 10 days of delivery to be desirable, 20 to be marginally acceptable. From 1974 through 1976, no friendly broker averaged better than a 16-day delay in paying his bill. The delays apparently cost the company thousands of dollars in lost interest.[8]

And if a broker needed money to make a deal, there was no need to risk his own. In 1974, John R. Adams made a $2 million speculative purchase of gasoline from OKC in hopes of selling to a buyer for a profit. On the surface, the deal seemed ordinary, but a closer look revealed some interesting and unusual facts. In this case, Adams didn't risk a dime of his own money but borrowed the entire amount from the Fourth National Bank of Tulsa, Oklahoma. Cloyce Box was a director at that bank. Not only that, Box bought $2 million in certificates of deposit to secure the loan and pledged to buy back any of the gasoline that Adams did not sell.

When the note came due, Adams still hadn't found a buyer, so Box arranged for the loan to be refinanced through Mercantile National Bank of Dallas whose president conveniently sat on OKC's board of directors. Again, OKC put up the security and pledged to buy back the gasoline if necessary. The broker took no risk at all. OKC and Cloyce Box were on the hook for the whole amount.[9]

Some of the more controversial deals with Box's friendly brokers took place at the end of the fiscal year. For example, in 1974 OKC artificially boosted its year-end sales figure by selling large amounts of gasoline to two friendly brokers without delivering the gasoline or receiving any money for the sale until the following summer. It was a paper transaction only, apparently made for the purpose of making the company look better to investors and shareholders.

That same year, OKC bought 289,000 barrels of petroleum products from a friendly broker just days before it was time to close the books. Eighteen days later, after the books were closed, the company sold the petroleum products back to the same broker at the exact same price.[10]

Not that these kinds of transactions are necessarily illegal. Oil and gas sitting in a storage facility, like pork bellies hanging in a Chicago meat locker or corn piled high in a Midwest grain elevator, may change hands a dozen times without moving. Such transactions are legitimate as long as the commodities really exist, title to them actually changes hands, and all buyers and sellers are fully exposed to market fluctuations.

But the questions remain: Why would a company do business this way? What was the purpose of the friendly brokers? Was Box rewarding his friends by putting them in a position to take sky-high commissions? Was the friendly broker system a legitimate business tool, or was there a sinister purpose as some investigators and OKC stockholders suggested?

Box would call it "just doing business," but his personal enemies, and his old adversaries in Washington, speculated that the only possible explanation for such actions was that he was dodging federal regulations by selling gasoline and diesel to his friendly brokers at controlled prices and then taking secret and illegal kickbacks for himself after his brokers made huge sums of money reselling the products at a higher, unregulated price. What was potentially worse, Box continued the practice even after price controls were lifted.

The accusations prompted the Securities and Exchange Commission (SEC, a government agency that enforces securities laws and prosecutes individuals and companies that have committed fraud) to launch a full-scale investigation into Box's business affairs.

Even some of Box's closest friends took sides against him. When Boots Adams died in 1975, his family inherited 1.1 million shares of OKC stock, amounting to about 22 percent of the company. Three of Boots' sons, Gary, Steve, and Ken, sat on OKC's board of directors. Gary Adams took issue with Box's use of the friendly brokers.[11]

Some in the Box camp believed Gary Adams had personal reasons for taking a stand against Box. "What looked like a battle between my father and the SEC was really a battle between my father and the Adams brothers over control of the company," Doug Box explained. "They owned twice as much of the company as my father did, and they wanted to run it. They used the feds to attack my father and try to bring him down."[12]

"Not so," says Gary Adams. "I was on the board, and I had a responsibility to the shareholders. I heard that Cloyce was selling to some friends at market price and they were reselling the stuff at a higher price. I went down to Dallas to see if that was happening, and it was."[13]

More doubts about the friendly broker system came from David Ownby, a former vice president and chief salesman for OKC Trading Company (one of many OKC Corp. subsidiaries). Ownby would later testify in a pre-trial hearing before the SEC that he first suspected Box of acting illegally when Box had advised him

(Ownby) that the J. R. Adams Oil Company of Guymon, Oklahoma, was making a profit of fifty cents a barrel on resales of heavy industrial fuel oil purchased from OKC. However, a few months later, Ownby learned in a casual conversation with an Adams Oil customer that the real profit was $1.60 a barrel. If the same markup was applied to all of Adams's purchases that year, Ownby calculated Adams's undisclosed profits at over $1 million.

Ownby testified that the discovery cost him "a lot of sleep," because "Cloyce Box was like a father, to me and I knew there was something going on between the chairman of our company and a broker."[14]

Meanwhile, Gary Adams persuaded OKC's board of directors to launch an internal investigation into the friendly broker system. The investigation, conducted by the Dallas law firm of Locke, Purnell, Boren, Laney, and Neely, produced a three-volume report that explored allegations that Cloyce Box had engaged in a series of business transactions that benefitted him and a group of friends at the company's expense.

The Locke/Purnell report questioned Box's methods but absolved him of criminal activity. The report described a "perplexing problem" in finding a "logical and clear explanation" for the friendly broker system but found that "no legally actionable wrongs had occurred."[15] That was the end of the matter as far as the board of directors was concerned.

"I saw what Cloyce was doing, and I presented it to the board," Adams said. "But the board didn't have a problem with it."[16]

In the meantime, Adams gave copies of the Locke/Purnell Report to David Ownby and Tom Patrick, OKC's credit manager.[17] Ownby, whose job (in part) was federal compliance, showed his copy of the report to DOE investigators. Then one week later, Ownby and Patrick drove to Fort Worth and handed over the confidential report to agents at the SEC regional office.

Patrick feared retaliation for blowing the whistle on OKC and asked the SEC for anonymity. (Ownby had already resigned.) Responding to Patrick's concerns, SEC attorneys brought the two men into the federal courthouse in Dallas through a back entrance to a secret meeting with District Judge Patrick Higginbothom where Ownby and Patrick told the judge of several instances in which "lucrative offers to buy oil refined by OKC were rejected by Cloyce Box in favor of continued reliance on the friendly brokers at substantially lower sales prices."[18]

Patrick again expressed concerns for his job. He told the judge that two employees who had cooperated with the Locke/Purnell investigators had already been fired, and that he feared the same fate. As it turned out, that fear was justified.[19]

In addition to the SEC, the DOE launched an investigation into the alleged fee-sharing arrangements at OKC, and in its initial report, sent to the Justice Department, the DOE charged Cloyce Box with receiving "substantial kickbacks" from John R. Adams in return for brokerage concessions.

The report charged that in July 1973, Cloyce Box and John R. Adams agreed that "each was to pay the other a sales commission of 50% of the profits from any business opportunity referred to him by the other." To back up that claim, the report stated that Adams realized a $4.6 million profit on resales of OKC products in 1974 and that he "secretly paid sales commissions to Box totaling slightly over $2 million in the same year." An examination of Box's federal income tax return for 1974 showed that he received $1.9 million, plus an additional $35,000, in "petroleum product sales commissions."[20]

Cloyce Box's unconventional business practices were also the target of probes by the Justice Department and a Federal Grand Jury based in Oklahoma, but white-collar crimes are notoriously hard to prove.[21] It takes more than just unusual business behavior to build a case.

Were the friendly brokers created for a legitimate business purpose? Were they exposed to the ups and downs of the marketplace? Or were they created to evade government regulations and defraud company stockholders?

Some hint of Box's complex master plan could be found in the case of Don Baxter, a former OKC officer/director and one of Box's friendly brokers. In December 1973, when OKC complied with the FTC ruling by selling Jahncke Services Inc. of New Orleans, Baxter quit his job at OKC and bought Jahncke—with money he borrowed from Cloyce Box. "There are some indications," said the report of federal investigators, "that one of the reasons for permitting Mr. Baxter to broker OKC products may have been to assist him in paying off the note to OKC."[22]

The whole system, according to federal regulators, was nothing more than an elaborate scheme to funnel money back to Cloyce Box illegally.

Box fiercely defended his unusual business practices in the press saying, "the corporation needed trustworthy people to handle its marketing." There was, he said, nothing odd or underhanded about his business deals. It was the oil business and the complex federal regulations that were strange.[23]

He often cited strong profits at OKC as evidence that his actions were good for the company, and it is certainly true that OKC chalked up some of the largest profit margins in company history during the mid-1970s. Profits were up 19% in 1974, 12% in 1975, and 9% in 1976 compared to an average of less than 2% during the period from 1970 to 1972 when OKC was fighting Phillips Petroleum in court. Box spared no expense to defend himself, and for his money, he got the best talent in the business. He retained the services of Austin attorney Arthur Mitchell as lead counsel and old friend Hugh Aynesworth to deal with the press.

Arthur Mitchell, Box's classmate at Baylor Law School, was an aggressive and confrontational attorney who specialized in fighting government regulators. Mitchell was a spitfire and proud of it.

"If corporate lawyers are obnoxious, it's usually peripheral obnoxiousness," he declared. "It's not based on real, substantive contentiousness that comes from years of being a sonuvabitch."[24]

Aynesworth was a seasoned journalist and investigative reporter who once worked for Box and Fuller Construction in the early 1960s. Aynesworth was one of the few eyewitnesses to both the Kennedy assassination and the killing of Lee Harvey Oswald. Among his many journalistic accomplishments: he interviewed John F. Kennedy in the shower and played basketball with Fidel Castro.

At the suggestion of Hugh Aynesworth, Cloyce Box gave his side of the story to Andrew Sansom, a writer for *Texas Monthly Magazine*.

"The Adams kids (Gary, Ken, and Steve)," Box told Samson, "want the company for themselves as a base for their own operations. . . . They are all in their twenties, and they've never even run a gas station. Their strategy—and there's no secret about it; they told me what they were going to do—was to force an investigation and take the results to the board of directors. If they didn't win there, they'd take it to the FEA (Federal Energy Administration). If they didn't win there, they'd take it to the SEC (Securities and Exchange Commission). If they didn't win there, they'd take it to *Texas Monthly*. This investigation never should have happened. The regulatory process is being subverted to help one faction against another."[25]

Gary Adams insisted he never wanted to take over the company but believed some unethical, and possibly illegal, deals were being made. He was only doing what was best for the company by exercising his rights as a stockholder and board member.[26]

Box tried to explain to *Texas Monthly* his reasons for establishing the friendly broker system. His refinery was producing much more gasoline and diesel than it had in 1972, and OKC could either sell the excess directly to the major oil companies, wait for the DOE to assign customers, or choose its own new customers. After the fallout with Phillips, and especially after the near disaster at Fuller, Cloyce Box preferred not to do business with the majors, and at a time when the petroleum industry was in a state of upheaval, he reasoned that it made good sense to do business with friends.

A statement from OKC management explained, "the brokers provided the most efficient means of distributing refined products." The statement also claimed that OKC couldn't afford to hire salesmen of the same caliber, and the brokers "could entertain large customers in a manner that could not be tolerated in a publicly-held company."[27]

Box further explained that since refiners' profits were controlled, OKC couldn't have made any more money by eliminating the brokers. OKC, Box contended, was able to use the brokers and still extract the maximum profit the regulations allowed.

And finally, Box argued that once the brokers were approved as customers, federal regulations *required* OKC to sell them a certain amount of fuel every month. What Box didn't say was that the regulations only bind a company like OKC if the customers asked for their monthly quotas. In this case, the friendly brokers didn't call OKC. OKC called them.[28]

Despite Box's explanation, the friendly broker system was complicated and mysterious, and to a casual observer it had a hard time passing the smell test.

"Cloyce Box was right when he said OKC couldn't have made more money bypassing the friendly brokers," Norman Smith, Box's attorney, explained. "That was true in the beginning. Oil prices were fixed by the federal government by a complicated formula based on the national average price of old and new oil."

"Gulf was selling us (OKC) 15,000 barrels a day of old oil. Old oil prices were lower. Other companies could sell their new oil products at higher prices, but at OKC we sold old oil products and were locked into a lower price. We were selling our products at the maximum allowed by the government."

"And it wasn't just OKC using friendly brokers," Smith said. "Lots of companies were doing similar things. Everybody was trying to make money. But Cloyce had a history of fighting with the SEC, so they were watching him."

"Yes the friendly brokers made money. Some of them made a lot of money. But there was nothing illegal going on. The company was not hurt by the friendly broker system as long as price controls were in place."

"Then the brokers got greedy. They would sell products back and forth among themselves to jack up the price. They were difficult to deal with."

"And the friendly broker system should have stopped after price controls were lifted," Norman Smith stated, "but it didn't. It went on too long."[29]

Box's legal battle with the SEC and the DOE came at a frightful cost. Arthur Mitchell said he didn't know the exact figure but estimated the bill was "monstrous."[30]

The tremendous cost may have been a factor in a surprising move that took place on July 17, 1980. On that day, Box shocked everyone when he pled guilty to twenty-three misdemeanor violations of the DOE's pricing regulations.[31]

But Box got something important in return. In exchange for the guilty plea, he received a letter from the DOE stating all other charges had been dropped, and the Oklahoma grand jury investigation into his affairs had been "closed."

As a part of the settlement, OKC Corp. paid more than $5 million in civil penalties and agreed to forgo $20 million in future allowable increases. Box himself paid a fine of $620,000.

John R. Adams pled guilty to twenty counts of violating DOE pricing rules and paid a $100,000 fine. Friendly brokers Robert Whitley Sr. and Edwin W. Gummelt Jr. pled guilty to three charges each and paid fines of $15,000. Whitley and Gummelt were principals in Ritco Co., an organization the SEC charged with entering into "sham" transactions with Box and OKC. In yet another sinister twist in the case, the SEC claimed Box was a "hidden" 50 percent shareholder in Ritco, and in effect, he was "self-dealing," by entering into sham contracts with himself.[32]

The penalties from the settlement were "among the largest ever obtained for violations under the oil-pricing program," stated Larry D. Patton, US Attorney for the Western District of Oklahoma.[33]

But in the long run, Patton's speech rang hollow. The prosecutor clearly wanted more, but a string of misdemeanor violations was all he could get. If the illegal profits were anywhere close to the amounts alleged by the DOE, the fines were, as they say in Texas, "chicken feed."

What irritated government regulators was Box's reaction to the settlement. Instead of acting contrite, he talked like a winner. His attorneys maintained that the twenty-three misdemeanor violations were nothing more than misinterpretations and minor oversights. Cloyce Box and OKC had done nothing wrong.

At the conclusion of the case, Robert Miller, an OKC company spokesman, issued the following unrepentant statement. "In effect, we said, 'we didn't do it, and we won't do it again.'"[34]

Box likely had compelling reasons for settling with the DOE. He was battling the DOE and the SEC at the same time, and he most certainly settled with the DOE to concentrate his efforts against the more serious allegations he knew were forthcoming from the SEC.

The SEC was doubly motivated to go after Box. Its agents loathed Box since the Jahncke days, and could hardly wait to get him into court.

"It is now utterly clear," an SEC spokesperson said, "that because of the flagrant ongoing violations, and the defendants' attempts to frustrate a lawful commission investigation, a preliminary injunction should be issued to protect the public interest."[35]

Sure enough, on September 16, 1980, just eight weeks after the DOE settlement, the SEC filed suit in Federal Court in Dallas charging Cloyce Box with engaging in a scheme that extended special treatment to his "friendly brokers" in exchange for secret and illegal "kickbacks and commissions" between 1974 and 1977.[36]

"The magnitude of the kickbacks by the 'friendly brokers' to Box is staggering," the SEC added.[37]

In a pretrial statement, SEC attorneys alleged that Cloyce Box "caused OKC to purchase and sell substantial amounts of petroleum products through brokers who were his friends and business associates, pursuant to secret and undisclosed partnership and business arrangements. It was also alleged that at Box's discretion, these friendly brokers received preferential price, product delivery, and credit arrangements from OKC and in turn, resold these products at substantial markup. At least two of these 'friendly brokers,' according to the complaint, then split their profits with Box.

"Pursuant to these arrangements, Box received in excess of $5 million over a four-year period. The Commission charged that none of the money was disclosed by OKC in its periodic, annual, or other reports. The SEC also alleged that Box used certain of these 'friendly brokers' as parties in fictitious purchases and sales of petroleum products in which OKC purportedly engaged, resulting in material falsification of OKC's interim and year-end financial statements."[38]

The lawsuit went on to say that Box and OKC went to great lengths to conceal the "enormous kickbacks" by, among other things, "vigorously resisting investigations by the SEC and the press and entering into a settlement last July with the Department of Energy over oil-pricing irregularities." According to the SEC, Box's sudden motivation to settle the DOE charges after years of resistance was to escape personal liability for the actions being investigated by the Security and Exchange Commission.

The complaint asked for a complete accounting of company transactions between 1973 and 1980, Box's resignation as CEO and director of OKC, and the return of any monies wrongfully diverted from the company.[39]

The charges were serious, but Cloyce Box was unconcerned. He had a plan to deal with his enemies at the SEC. No one saw it coming.

In 1971, OKC Corp. acquired 15.83 percent interest in a 2-million-acre oil and gas field in the Gulf of Guayaquil on the Pacific Coast of Ecuador. The field contained an estimated 4 trillion cubic feet of natural gas reserves.

That spring, a consortium of companies that included OKC, Phillips Petroleum, and Swift and Company began drilling an offshore well in the area. Ada Oil Company of Houston, owned by Boots Adams's son Bud Adams (a half-brother to Gary Adams and owner of the Houston Oilers—later the Tennessee Titans), did the drilling in 120 feet of water about twenty-five miles from shore.

"Cloyce Box was there before any of them," remembered Maurice Campbell, Box's attorney and friend. "He was the first American oil man in Ecuador. He had no fear, and he negotiated the deal just like always. He liked to deal face to face with the head man, and that's what he did. He believed he could negotiate with anybody. He went straight to the dictator and negotiated the lease to drill. Nobody had done that before—ever."[40]

The military dictator of Ecuador, General Guillermo Rodriquez Lara, was proficient in English, having studied Irregular Warfare Orientation and Maintenance Management at the School of the Americas in Panama. His nickname was "Bombita" (light bulb).

Cloyce Box soon discovered that dealing with a South American dictator was not fundamentally different from dealing with changing whims and enlarged egos of American CEOs. In either case, it is best to guard your backside. And just because an agreement was written down, didn't make it so. The difference was that in the United States, business disputes were resolved in the courthouse and political differences were reconciled at the ballot box. In Ecuador, disputes in both business and politics were often settled with airplanes, tanks, and guns.

"One of OKC's Ecuador leases was in the jungle—a very difficult environment," Maurice Campbell recalled. "It rains 200 inches a year there in some of the world's most difficult conditions. Roads don't ex-

ist. I don't know that any company ever drilled a well under those conditions before. But no problem was too tough for Cloyce Box. Do you know how he solved it? It's really an amazing story."

"He bought a brand new helicopter and a new bulldozer. Then he hired a local man from Ecuador who knew the forest. He swung that man on a lanyard beneath that helicopter and dropped him in the jungle at the well site. 'I'll see you in two weeks,' Cloyce told him. The man had food, water, and a machete, and his job was to clear a path from the well site to the coast."

"Cloyce then had his men take the new bulldozer apart and ship it on barges to the coast of Ecuador piece by piece. On the beach in Ecuador, the men put the dozer back together, found the man who hacked his way out of the jungle, and used the dozer to clear the road to the well site. The rig was shipped in pieces by barge to the coast and then trucked up the road to the well."[41]

OKC Corp. spudded its first well on the mainland of Ecuador in August 1972, on its lease in the Oriente region in the eastern foothills of the Andes Mountains in northeast Ecuador. Someone at OKC dubbed the well "Caja No. 1." Caja is Spanish for "box."

The lease arrangement appeared to be a good deal for Ecuador and for Box. Campbell recalled that "Cloyce's company did all the work and took all the risks, while Ecuador got a certain amount of money for each barrel of oil produced. The lease also gave Cloyce the right to take oil from the site for twenty years; then the site went back to Ecuador."

"But what the leader of Ecuador really wanted was Cloyce's new helicopter."

"Few people thought Cloyce could get his chopper out of there because the dictator always got what he wanted. But the dictator had never dealt with Cloyce Box."

"He [Box] solved the problem just like he solved every problem that came along in his life. He made a plan and followed it. Cloyce gave the helicopter pilot a handful of $100 bills and a map and said, 'I'll see you in a few days.' Do you know what the pilot did? He short hopped his way out of Ecuador all the way to Frisco, Texas, stopping along the way anywhere he could to buy gas. Five days later he landed on the infield at Cloyce's horse track next to the big ranch house in Frisco."[42]

Box kept his chopper, but wasn't so lucky with his South American oil concessions. The next year, Ecuador joined OPEC and voided its leases with OKC.

14

Six Feet Four and Bulletproof

The question isn't who is going to let me;
it's who is going to stop me.

—Ayn Rand

In May 1980, OKC stockholders received a letter from the director and CEO announcing plans to liquidate the company, sell its assets, and go out of business. In the letter, Cloyce Box urged stockholders to approve the plan because liquidation would yield them more than they "may reasonably expect to obtain through the normal market transactions for OKC common stock."[1]

OKC's assets at the time, listed in the company's annual report for the fiscal year ending September 20, 1979, amounted to $114 million. According to the liquidation plan, company assets would be sold as soon as possible to interested companies with all assets to be liquidated by July 1981. The money that remained after paying all debts would be distributed to shareholders.[2]

On the matter of liquidation, there were at least two different opinions. Some shareholders thought the liquidation plan made sound financial sense in light of recent developments, but Box's enemies saw the plan as a scheme by Box to beat the Securities and Exchange Commission and hold on to the money he had obtained through illegal transactions.

As one oil analyst said, "It's tough to make charges stick against a non-existent company."[3]

Box scheduled a shareholder meeting in Dallas on May 13, 1980, to gain approval for his liquidation plan. At about the same time, a reporter for the *Wall Street Journal* wrote an article, based on a leaked copy of the Locke/Purnell report, that the paper scheduled for publication on the same day as the OKC stockholders' meeting. Cloyce Box found out about the article and filed a lawsuit to keep it from being published, claiming that publication would violate OKC's Fourth Amendment rights.[4]

Up to that point, Box had been able to conceal the details of the Locke/Purnell report from most OKC stockholders. Only the board of directors, a handful of company executives, and a few others knew its contents.

Box wanted to keep it that way. He was concerned that if stockholders learned of the information contained in the *Wall Street Journal* article (information about the friendly brokers and about questionable financial practices), they might turn against him and foil his plan to dissolve the company and distribute its assets. Stockholders might even see the liquidation plan as a scheme by Cloyce Box to hold on to money gained by unusual, possibly illegal, business activities.

In an effort to stop the article from being published, Box and his legal team went on the offensive. They went after the *Wall Street Journal* with a vengeance.

Five days before the stockholder's meeting in Dallas, Arthur Mitchell went to court asking for a temporary restraining order barring the publication of the article on the grounds that the reporter obtained the Locke/Purnell report illegally (a violation of the Fourth Amendment right against illegal seizure), that the story would hurt the company in "certain pending publications and litigations," that attorney-client privilege would be destroyed, and that some twenty OKC lawsuits currently in litigation would be mooted by publication of the *Wall Street Journal* article.[5]

No one in the press seemed to think Mitchell's request stood a chance, but in an extremely controversial ruling, State District Judge Joe Fish sided with Box's attorneys and issued a temporary restraining order, placing the Locke/Purnell report under court seal until the following Friday, causing the *Wall Street Journal* to put publication of the article on hold.

The restraining order was unusual because until that time, nearly all successful attempts to restrain publication of a newspaper or magazine article had been brought by government officials—claiming that publication of government documents would breach national security (the *Pentagon Papers*, for example). A request for a restraining order made by a private business against a newspaper was usually deemed contrary to public interest (the thought being that the company had something to hide) and was rarely issued.[6]

It is interesting to note that the *Wall Street Journal* was not even represented at the hearing that caused the restraining order to be issued and the newspaper did not find out about it until after the order was served.[7]

As expected, the *Journal* quickly denounced the restraining order as unconstitutional, and newspapers across the country rushed to condemn the judge's ruling. One editor wrote, "If a court can tell a newspaper not to publish certain information known to be heading for print—and can make it stick—then a once-free country's supposedly free people are close to a condition they never bargained for: governed by authorities with power to stop criticism of their acts of themselves through a 'prior restraint' of the press."[8]

Another paper quoted Thomas Jefferson. "When the press is free and every man able to read, all is safe."

The restraining order remained in effect through the weekend. Then on Monday, May 12, 1980, the judge heard arguments from lawyers representing the *Wall Street Journal*. For ninety minutes, the attorneys argued that the real objective of Box's legal efforts was to stall the SEC investigation, suppress litigation, and keep information in the Locke/Purcell report from becoming public.[9]

Box, the lawyers suggested, needed stockholder approval to liquidate the company in order to keep his illegal kickbacks, but the information contained in the *Wall Street Journal* article might cause a majority of stockholders to oppose Box's plan.

After the hearing, the judge reversed himself and dissolved the restraining order.

The article hit the streets the next day, May 13, 1980—the same day as the OKC stockholders meeting. The article appeared on page one and quoted a Box attorney as saying that he "is facing imminent indictment" for charging "friendly" brokers too little for refined oil products and for taking kickbacks and for other criminal violations of federal securities laws. The article also claimed that Box and OKC were "engaged in a strenuous campaign to fight and even suppress allegations that he and certain associates were involved in a number of questionable transactions with OKC."[10]

The article claimed that Box initiated a multitude of lawsuits in state and federal court for no other purpose than to impede and forestall investigations by the SEC and the DOE. Another objective of the lawsuits was to keep confidential the findings of the Locke/Purnell report.

The article hinted that Box's brazen behavior was unprecedented in the history of business and called his campaign of suppression "unique in the annals of publically held companies."[11]

But in the end, the article that Cloyce Box fought so hard to suppress had no noticeable impact on the meeting in Dallas. OKC stockholders, many of whom carried copies of the *Wall Street Journal* under their arms, instructed the board of directors to sell off the company's assets, pay its debts, and go out of business. The vote to liquidate was 400 to 1. Not a single question about the *Wall Street Journal* article came up at the meeting.[12]

Box was vindicated, at least by his company shareholders. It is interesting to note that as soon as the *Wall Street Journal* article, based on the Locke/Purnell report, hit the streets, OKC stock rose one and one-half to $49 per share.

While Cloyce Box hotly denied the allegations made by the *Wall Street Journal*, Arthur Mitchell filed still more actions against the SEC. One of the lawsuits asked for $15 million in damages allegedly inflicted by the government's investigation of OKC.

The principal character in the lawsuit was Ghaith R. Pharaon, a shady Saudi Arabian businessman with corrupt connections to the US government at the highest levels. Pharaon was a business partner of Bert Lance, President Jimmy Carter's disgraced budget director, and former Texas Governor and former US Secretary of the Treasury John Connally.[13] Pharaon also had a loose business connection to world-renowned terrorist and al-Qaeda leader Osama bin Laden.

In 1979, Pharaon announced his intention to buy 950,000 shares of OKC stock at $21 a share—15% above the trading price—but withdrew his offer after meeting with SEC officials in Washington, DC. Cloyce Box and Mitchell believed the SEC "intentionally sabotaged" the deal, but government officials maintained that the agency made no effort to dissuade Pharaon from buying OKC stock.[14]

The courts eventually threw out most of Box's lawsuits, although one newspaper reported that the legal actions did buy him enough time to locate and fire the employee who leaked the Locke/Purnell report to the SEC.

On February 2, 1979, OKC's personnel manager and company lawyer handed a letter to Tom Patrick. The letter was official notification that Patrick had been fired. The attorney then took the company car keys and escorted Patrick out of the building.

When asked for an explanation, Arthur Mitchell told the press "We ain't running over any little people, but we can't operate with a pipeline to the SEC sitting in the next office."[15]

Tom Patrick paid the price for disloyalty. Unable to find a job in the petroleum industry because of his notoriety as an SEC informant, he bought a hamburger stand in Dallas.[16]

Arthur Mitchell became an expert at fighting government regulators using the tactic of delay. Twenty times the SEC issued subpoenas for OKC records, and each time, Mitchell challenged the subpoenas in court on the grounds that they were unconstitutional and overly broad. He brought in seven separate law firms for support. He dragged the SEC through twelve courtrooms before nine different judges in three states. Twice he went to the US Supreme Court and three times to the Fifth Circuit Court.

Mitchell was proud that he forced the SEC to battle for every scrap of information.

"I didn't give 'em nuthin'," he said.[17]

The SEC got the cold shoulder wherever it turned. Even the banks were uncooperative with SEC investigators. Faced with silent threats of large withdrawals, five banks with close ties to OKC and with records relevant to the investigation also challenged SEC subpoenas.

That kind of action was not unexpected. "How long do you think we would be in business if we didn't challenge these subpoenas?" said one bank official who asked not to be identified. At the same time, at least a dozen of Box's business associates refused on Fifth Amendment grounds to answer any questions by SEC investigators.[18]

As a result of the challenges, the SEC spent 15 months simply trying to obtain documents from OKC, Cloyce Box, the brokers, and the banks.[18] Only when Federal Judge Patrick E. Higginbotham of the Federal District Court in Dallas ordered OKC to comply with the subpoenas did the company produce the documents the federal government spent over a year trying to obtain, and only then could the real investigation begin.

"The company has had us tied up in legal knots for 15 months," reported Michael J. Stewart, director of the Fort Worth Regional Office of the SEC. It was "massive, monumental" resistance.

"This is our worst enforcement mess ever," said Roberta S. Karmel, an SEC commissioner.[19]

Of course, frustrating the SEC was exactly what Box had set out to do, and it worked. One SEC employee said, "Their [Box and Mitchell's] tactics have been obstructionist, brought in bad faith, and have been totally frivolous. Yet the fact is they were very successful."[20]

After an exhaustive investigation, including interviews with the friendly brokers, a close examination of OKC tax records, and a court battle that lasted five years, the court found Cloyce Box guilty of only one count: the relatively minor crime of illegally paying the fees of his personal attorney in the case with corporate funds. As punishment, US District Judge Robert M. Hill ordered Box to pay $1 million to OKC's liquidating trust. Box and OKC agreed to the order, without admitting or denying the allegations in the Commission's complaint.[21] The court also dismissed the charges against Box.

Box, in effect, had beaten the SEC or at least fought it to a draw. He got a slap on the wrist and paid a small fine.

Try as they may, SEC attorneys could never prove their most serious allegation: that Cloyce Box received personal income off the books for at least seven years through illegal transactions, kickbacks, and commissions involving OKC and the "friendly" brokers.

The SEC appealed the verdict to the Fifth Circuit Court, but the high court upheld the verdict of the lower court. With that ruling, all litigation between OKC and the SEC ended.

And Box won another battle that was just as important as the standoff in the courtroom. While he remained a villain to government regulators, in business circles, he was a hero. Many company executives all over America openly cheered Box and OKC for their stand against the SEC and the federal government. Those supporters reflected a general feeling in corporate America that the SEC had "gotten too big for its britches," and many corporate executives were elated that the SEC had been "taken down a notch."

The evidence suggests that the battle between Box and the SEC changed forever the relationship between business and government. Before the "friendly brokers" court battle, regulatory agencies had the upper hand. SEC attorneys might go to court with a weak case because businesses had a tendency to settle rather than risk a fight with the SEC.

Many corporate executives believed a fight with the SEC was a kiss of death. Just the prospect of an investigation brought disruptions and adverse publicity. Even if you won in the end, you were bled white by the battle.

But Cloyce Box and Arthur Mitchell changed the game and tipped the scale in favor of private enterprise. Now the prospect of a legal donnybrook made the SEC and other regulatory agencies think twice before going on a fishing expedition. In the future, the SEC would call its shots more carefully.[22]

For proof that Box and Mitchell made the right move in going after the SEC, one had only to look at stock prices. OKC stock that had been selling around the $15 mark was suddenly selling at over $70 a share. By the end of January 1981, the price of OKC stock was 84½. One month later, the price was $106. On March 1, 1981, OKC stocks jumped 32¾ points to 126¾. On March 15, 1981, OKC stock soared 21 points to 138¾. The company issued a press release saying it had no explanation for the rise in prices.

Then over the summer, prices fell back to levels that were more realistic. On August 21, 1981, the market closed with OKC shares selling at $87.75. The company paid a $15 a share dividend on preferred stock for the previous fiscal year.

Box knew that stockholders and the market responded to sure, aggressive leadership and that possible unethical behavior, even possible illegal behavior, could be overlooked by investors and company directors as long as profits were high. He knew who buttered his bread.

"The name of the game is to make money," Box told a journalist. "I don't care what the SEC or Mr. Stewart (director of the SEC office in Fort Worth) think of me. I have stockholders who paid $4 a share for OKC stock now selling in the 70s. They think well of me."[23]

"Cloyce had a way of doing things," Gary Adams remembered years later, "and it was his way. He definitely looked out for himself, but I always liked him. We had our differences, but it was all out in the open. We laid everything on the table. Nothing was hidden. And it was never personal. It was just business."[24]

The impersonal nature of some oil business litigation is hard for most people to understand. For most of us, lawsuits are filed in anger. Going to court is a bitter, unpleasant experience. But to Cloyce Box and his associates, lawsuits were just a part of doing business. They were strictly routine, like flow charts and board meetings.

What separated Cloyce Box from other businessmen was how quickly he filed suit, how often he relied on the courtroom to settle business disputes, and how much he enjoyed the battle.

"Cloyce never shied away from litigation," Gary Adams recalled. "He loved it. He loved the fight. He wasn't right all the time, but he was not afraid to take on anyone. And we could walk out of the courtroom and still be civil."[25]

"In Cloyce's defense the rules weren't exactly clear as to what you could and could not do," David Ownby explained. "I believe Cloyce crossed the line, so I left. I believe he was circumventing the system. That's unfortunate. But even though we had a falling out I still respected him."[26]

After the OKC Board of Directors approved the liquidation plan, the company put its assets on the market including two cement plants, the Okmulgee refinery, and the dredging business in Louisiana. On September 5, 1980, Lone Star Industries agree to buy OKC's cement plant and dock facility in New Orleans for $50 million. On January 2, 1981, Basin Refining Inc. of Midland, Texas, bought OKC's Okmulgee Refinery for $115.4 million then defaulted six months later after paying out $77 million.[27] The plant resold for $84 million.[28]

Then on May 11, 1981, OKC Corp. completed liquidation except for its valuable oil and gas properties, which were spun off to form a new company called OKC-LP (for limited partnership). The shareholders of OKC Corp. became limited partners in OKC-LP. Instead of liquidating completely as planned, Box's oil company was back in business under a new name.[29]

As usual with Box and his organization, nothing was simple or as it appeared to be. A company called CKB and Associates became the temporary general partners (day-to-day operators) of OKC-LP. Another entity called Box Brothers Holding Company owned 94 percent of CKB and Associates. Cloyce Box owned and controlled Box Brothers Holding Company, making him the majority owner and chief operating office of all three companies.[30]

On October 19, 1981, OKC-LP held a partnership meeting in Dallas to obtain approval of Cloyce Box and CKB and Associates as permanent general partners. At the meeting, the shareholders gave their consent to the arrangement and approved an agreement stating that "all authority to act on behalf of the Partnership is vested in the General Partners" and with limited exceptions, the general partners "have complete and exclusive discretion in the management and control of the Partnership."[31]

After the SEC troubles were over and Box's leadership of OKC-LP was affirmed, Box felt like a winner. He had been vindicated and could barely contain his delight. He was 6 feet 4 and bulletproof.

In just over a year, Box had accomplished what some thought impossible. He had beaten the SEC, dissolved his old company, and formed a new company with himself as CEO.

"I just figure it was a fair fight, and I won," he boldly declared. "I never invite trouble, and I never run from it."[32]

Doug Box described his father as "honed by hardship and adversity into a powerhouse businessman. He had a remarkable business career that was surrounded by controversy. He was fearless and aggressive, and he played hard. He got where he was in life by playing hard. That's how he did business because that was all he knew. That's how he did everything. You have to remember he learned to operate in a pre-Watergate era. He was always pushing the envelope. He never learned to relax, and he never let up. In those days there were a lot of powerful flamboyant businessmen who played fast and loose with the rules, and in most cases they could get by with it, if they didn't go too far. That was the business culture of the time. That's how business was done. My father was a part of that fraternity."

"And he liked corporate warfare. He was energized by it."

"He believed he was entitled to wealth and power because he could do something good with it. He used his wealth and power to create jobs and more wealth. That's how he justified it."[33]

"But something happened to him after he fought the SEC to a draw," Doug Box added. "The incident gave him a false sense of confidence that would one day contribute to his downfall. He had gotten away with something and was emboldened by it. He had dodged a bullet, and he felt invincible. After he stared down the SEC, he wasn't afraid of anything."[34]

No one could close a deal with the cold-blooded flair of Cloyce Box. He made Donald Trump look like a shoe salesman.

On July 15, 1982, Box signed an agreement to supply Texas Eastern Transmission Company with natural gas from a field in the Gulf of Mexico. Texas Eastern owned and operated a pipeline that carried natural gas from the Gulf Coast to the northeastern United States. Box negotiated a 20-year contract with Texas Eastern at a time when natural gas prices were high, and no one could see prices going anywhere but up. Nor did anyone blink at a provision in the agreement that called for 10% yearly price increases for the duration of the contract.

Officials at Texas Eastern thought they were protecting themselves from an energy-starved world of steadily higher natural gas prices. Instead, new fields were discovered, and gas prices promptly sank 35%.

Within a few months, the price of natural gas had dropped so low that all the other Texas Eastern suppliers agreed to renegotiate the price they charged—but not Cloyce Box. He went to court to enforce the current contract. Ten years later, Texas Eastern Transmission Company still paid Box $9 per 1,000 cubic foot for natural gas when the spot price was less than $2.[35]

15

Brought Down by a French Fry

Money lent to a friend must be recovered from an enemy.

—German Proverb

For years, geologists predicted there were rich petroleum deposits beneath the Gulf of Mexico, but drilling technology did not exist to bring that petroleum to the surface. Onshore methods did not always transfer to offshore drilling.

The biggest problem was that offshore wells needed a stable platform for the drilling rig. The earliest platforms, built of wood, close to shore, and in less than twenty feet of water, showed limited success. They were expensive and vulnerable to infamous gulf coast hurricanes. Besides, most of the oil was in deeper water offshore.

In the late 1930s, Superior Oil (now ExxonMobil) had some success with a wooden platform about a mile off the Louisiana coast, but World War II interrupted its development.

After the war, a small Oklahoma company called Kerr-McGee (today Anadarko Petroleum) came up with a novel approach—using gutted World War II surplus LSTs as drill ships. LSTs were large seagoing vessels, about 300 feet long, designed to carry tanks and other heavy cargo directly onto the beach in support of amphibious landings. The LSTs were not the answer, but lessons learned from their use led to more sophisticated drill ships that came later.

The technology of drilling offshore continued to improve until, on November 14, 1947, Kerr-McGee (owned by Cloyce Box's Oklahoma friend Robert S. Kerr), acting as an operator for Phillips

Petroleum (now ConocoPhillips) and Standard Oil (now BP), brought in the first well out of sight of land: the Ship Shoal Block 32 well, forty-five miles south of Morgan City, Louisiana. The platform sat on steel legs in twenty-two feet of water.

The birth of the offshore oil and gas industry marked a new phase in the evolution of the petroleum business, transformed the coastlines of Louisiana, Mississippi, Alabama, and Texas, and provided an enormous new opportunity for oilmen, like Cloyce Box, who were ready and willing to take a risk.

Three years after the Ship Shoal Block 32 well came in, geologists discovered a monster oil and gas field in federal waters thirty-five miles off the Louisiana coast, just southeast of the mouth of the Mississippi River. Water depth in the field ranged from 140 to 190 feet. Although the field, called South Pass, was enormous, the expense of drilling there insured little activity in the area as long as onshore sites produced crude in sufficient quantities. Only when onshore production in easily accessible places began to decline, did expensive offshore wells became more cost-effective.

On July 1, 1967, Phillips Petroleum and its partners, Amerada-Hess, Marathon Oil, and Louisiana Land and Exploration, acquired from the US government a mineral lease giving each partner one-quarter working interest in South Pass. From the beginning, the field produced great quantities of oil and natural gas, except for a section called Block 89, and all geological evidence suggested that Block 89 had only marginal economic value.

From 1967 to 1977, Phillips and its partners drilled exploratory wells in Block 89 and determined that the area contained about 4 million barrels of crude in proven and potential reserves and another 4 million barrels with a poor possibility of recovery.

Based on that grim economic review, Phillips Petroleum and the other partners chose to cease operations in Block 89. For the giants, there did not appear to be enough petroleum down there to justify the expense of bringing it to the surface.

So, in the spring of 1977, the partners decided to sell their interests in Block 89 to a company willing to bear the construction costs of an oil platform in exchange for the acquisition of their interest in the Block 89 lease. On June 14, 1977, Phillips Petroleum and its partners farmed out their entire working interest in Block 89 to Cloyce Box and OKC Corp. Gary Adams did the negotiating for OKC.[1]

Box paid half a million dollars for the 13,000-acre lease on the outer Continental Shelf and fortunately for Box, the experts were wrong. There was more petroleum in Block 89 than anyone imagined. By the time of his death in 1993, Box's South Pass lease had produced 42 million barrels of oil and 67 billion cubic feet of natural gas.[2]

From 1982, when OKC-LP's first well in Block 89 came in, until March 1, 1985, OKC-LP transported its crude from its offshore rigs to a receiving station on the Louisiana shore via a pipeline owned by Marathon Oil. OKC-LP paid Marathon a tariff of $2.75 a barrel to use the pipeline.

As more rigs pumped more oil from the South Pass field, Box worried that his pipeline agreement with Marathon might not be renewed, or that the fee would increase, so on August 30, 1984, he offered to purchase a one-quarter interest in the pipeline for $4,757,000. He wanted to protect his company by securing capacity on the line. One week later, Marathon accepted the offer.

As soon as OKC-LP received official notification that the offer was accepted, the company notified Marathon that interest in the pipeline would not actually be purchased by OKC-LP but by an affiliate, a private company called CKB Petroleum. Box Brothers Holding Company owned 94.4 percent of CKB Petroleum, and Cloyce Box controlled Box Brothers Holding Company.[3] CKB Petroleum was in effect Box's private company.

Marathon did not wish to sell interest in the pipeline to CKB Petroleum and imposed an express condition on the sale that OKC-LP had to be the purchaser. Cloyce Box agreed, and the two companies closed the deal on February 28, 1985. On that day, OKC-LP paid the agreed purchase price. (Box actually borrowed the money from Trammell Crow through Manufacturers Hanover Trust Company.)

Then things got even more interesting. The day after the sale, Cloyce Box did what he wanted to do all along. OKC-LP transferred the rights of the pipeline to its affiliate, CKB Petroleum. There was nothing Marathon could do. The sale had already taken place.

As part of the agreement between OKC-LP and CKB Petroleum (an agreement between Cloyce Box and himself), CKB Petroleum agreed to make available to OKC-LP all of its pipeline capacity for the next 20 years, and OKC-LP agreed to ship all of its oil produced in Block 89 through the pipeline. The parties also agreed to a fixed tariff of $2.75 per barrel for all oil shipped through the pipeline for the 20-year term of the agreement.

So, with a little corporate magic, a steady stream of pipeline tariff money began to flow from OKC-LP, a public company owned by stockholders, to CKB Petroleum, a private company owned by Cloyce Box. A March 1, 1985, letter broke the news of the pipeline transfer and the transportation charges to OKC-LP stockholders.[4]

The news was not well received. The transfer of the interest in the pipeline from the publically held company into private hands effectively shut out OKC-LP shareholders from any future profits from the pipeline and channeled all the earnings from the pipeline to CKB Petroleum and its owner—Cloyce Box.

A group of investors, led by Box's former friend, Idaho businessman J. R. Simplot, immediately filed suit. Simplot and his friends believed Cloyce Box defrauded OKC shareholders by selling the pipeline to himself at a bargain price, and then milked investors by charging them for its use. Simplot and his attorneys charged Box with securities fraud, federal racketeering, breach of contract, breach of fiduciary responsibility, and breach of good faith and fair dealing.[5]

Many people wondered why Cloyce Box would make such a daring and controversial move that he knew would be vigorously challenged in court. He never gave a reason in public, but speculation was rampant.

"I think he did it to protect the OKC stockholders from litigation," Box's friend Kent Hance said. "Oil spills were not unusual in the Gulf, and the lawsuits from one spill could bankrupt the company. If a spill occurred, he wanted the lawsuits aimed at him, not the company."[6]

Another possible explanation was that Box was planning to build a cement plant in Midlothian, Texas. The project would be costly (between $90 million and $100 million), and he may have needed the pipeline money to hedge his bet in Midlothian. The income from the pipeline may have been the only way he could manage the risk of the cement plant.

Whatever his reasons for transferring the pipeline to CKB Petroleum, Box had a tiger by the tail. J. R. Simplot was a little man, with a disarming personality, but he was no small fry. Simplot would dog his former friend to the grave and beyond.

"Cloyce Box and J. R. Simplot were a lot alike," Hance remembered. "They had similar personalities, and they clashed. When Simplot became a major stockholder at OKC, he thought he could tell Cloyce how to run the company. Cloyce didn't want his input."[7]

Box's attorney Norman Smith believed Simplot had a more sordid reason to go after Cloyce Box. It was all about greed.

"Simplot overpaid for a bunch of OKC-LP stock," said Smith. "For a period of several months, he was about the only one buying OKC-LP. He ran the price up to $30 a share. When he stopped buying there were no buyers left and the stock prices fell. He and his lawyers decided they needed to do something to recoup his losses, so they sued."[8]

The court battle between J. R. Simplot and the Box family for control of OKC-LP (later Box Energy) became part of business legend.

John Richard Simplot had been a brawler all his life. He grew up in Idaho in the 1920s and 1930s, and being an Idaho boy, he knew potatoes. In a hurry to make money, he dropped out of school in the eighth grade, and went to work as a farm laborer near Boise at age 14. Three years later, he bought 500 hogs for $500 in a depressed market. He dramatically cut the cost of fattening the animals by feeding them potato scraps and meat from wild horses he hunted on the open range. When the swine market came back, Simplot sold his hogs for $7,800. That rather modest sum became the foundation for a billion-dollar fortune.

Simplot used the profits from the hog sale to buy draft horses and farm machinery to raise potatoes on a rented farm. He learned everything there was to know about spuds, and at the age of thirty-five, by grit, street smarts, and force of personality, Simplot had amassed a fortune in agribusiness. He raised potatoes on his farm in Idaho, developed a process to slice them and quick-freeze them, and then sold them to Pillsbury and other food companies. Simplot pioneered the frozen French fry—a product ideally suited to the emerging fast-food industry.

Then in 1967, Simplot met legendary businessman Ray Kroc, founder of McDonalds, and in a contractual agreement sealed with only a handshake ("Not a damn lawyer in the room"), Simplot agreed to supply McDonalds restaurants with precut frozen French fries.

Before the meeting at Kroc's California ranch, all McDonald's fries were cut daily at the store level. The process was time consuming but necessary because Kroc was a stickler for quality. He had tried frozen French fries before, but they turned mushy when cooked. Kroc was also a stickler for consistency and was often unhappy with the quality of fresh potatoes, particularly during the summer months.

Then he tried a Simplot French fry, produced by the blanch, fry, and freeze technique perfected by a Simplot chemist, and was pleased with the taste and texture. Simplot's company still provides one-half of all McDonald's French fries worldwide. By 2006, Simplot was worth $2.6 billion and at ninety-six was the world's oldest billionaire.

J. R. Simplot did not take bad financial news well. When he heard about the pipeline transfer, he invited all disgruntled OKC-LP investors to a meeting at the LBJ Hilton Hotel in north Dallas. In the words of Box's attorney, "He (Simplot) got together all the people who thought they were being screwed."[9]

Simplot made it plain he wanted to throw Box out and plotted a course to dethrone him as managing general partner (CEO) of OKC-LP. (Box's removal by force would require court action or a majority vote by the board of directors.) A few weeks later, the Simplot group filed documents with the Texas Secretary of State announcing its intention to amend OKC-LP's partnership agreement and replace the general partners then in charge of the company.[10]

Meanwhile, Box had plans of his own. To counter Simplot's move, Box convened a meeting of the current OKC-LP Board of Directors, all friends of his who owed their jobs to him, and changed the written articles of the partnership making it harder for angry investors to remove him as CEO.

First, he dissolved OKC-LP and transferred its assets and liabilities to Box Energy Corp.—a newly formed Delaware corporation.[11] The new Box Energy Board of Directors included Cloyce K. Box, President, Chairman of the Board, and CEO; Don D. Box, Cloyce's son and President of CKB and Associates; Kent R. Hance, Box's friend and a partner in the law firm of Hance and Gamble of Austin, Texas; Nauman S. Scott III, a New Orleans Attorney and the brother of Ashley Scott who would become Box's second wife; and two old friends, NFL Hall of Famers, and Heisman Trophy winners: Roger Staubach, President of The Staubach Company of Dallas (real estate development) and Doak Walker, Vice President (retired) of Fishbach and Moore (an engineering firm). It was hard to deny that the friendly faces around the boardroom table gave Box a comfortable feeling and substantial home-court advantage.

Box and his board then wrote a new corporate charter that divided company stock into two categories—Class A stock and Class B stock—BOXXA and BOXXB on the Nasdaq.[12] Both categories of stock were entitled to equal participation in earnings, dividends, and liquidation proceeds, but there was an interesting and controversial provision. Only Class A stock had voting rights. Since Box personally owned 57% of the 3.2 million Class A voting shares, he controlled the company.

The Class A stockholders then held their own meeting in Dallas and voted overwhelmingly to reaffirm Cloyce Box as the CEO of the company. Since Box owned a majority of the Class A shares, the vote was a forgone conclusion.

At the same time Box countersued, claiming Simplot, his former friend and business partner, was scheming to usurp control of the company.[13]

The court battle dragged on for years. Lawyer fees and court costs were astronomical—more that the gross national products of some African countries. Some of the most famous law firms in America, including Fulbright and Jaworski; Hughes and Luce; and Vinson, Elkins, Searles, Connally, and Smith, paraded through the District Courtroom in Dallas representing one side or the other in the course of the long and costly litigation.

It is a testimony to the tenacity and fierce desire for vengeance of both Cloyce Box and J. R. Simplot that, years after Cloyce Box's death, the case was still not resolved. The court file weighed several hundred pounds and filled three long shelves in the US District Clerk's office in Dallas.[14]

Frustrated by slow progress of the criminal case, Simplot and five other OKC shareholders filed a civil suit against Box. Civil cases, involving private disputes between people or companies, are often easier to prove than criminal cases, which involve crimes that are harmful to society. This time, a jury found that Box had indeed violated his responsibilities to his shareholders and profited at the company's expense.

The jury awarded the Simplot group a $28 million settlement. Of great concern to Box was that the judgment was not just against the company. Box was personally liable.

The verdict, as you might expect, was not the end of the story. After a jury reaches its conclusion, the verdict must be formally approved (entered) by the presiding judge before it becomes official. In this case, District Judge Robert Maloney decided not to enter the verdict immediately, but gave the two sides some time to hash out a compromise—a move that surprised Simplot and his associates. They agreed to negotiate, but only because they worried that Judge Maloney might not uphold the verdict.

Another reason the Simplot group agreed to talk was a fear that Cloyce Box didn't have the money to pay the settlement. In 1987, Box built a $91 million cement plant in Midlothian, Texas, but he mortgaged everything he had to raise the money.

To make matters worse for Box, the economy was in recession. Construction was slow. Cement sales were down. His expensive new cement plant struggled to turn a profit.

At the moment, Cloyce Box's financial empire was on shaky ground. He had few liquid assets. If the $28 million judgment went through and Box declared insolvency, the plaintiffs might only get pennies on the dollar.[15]

The cold, hard facts forced Simplot and his group to meet with Box's representatives in Dallas to try to reach a compromise, but within minutes, negotiations hit a brick wall. The meeting ended with nothing accomplished.

Judge Maloney then suggested that an independent board of arbitration conduct an investigation and negotiate a settlement.

As CEO of the company, it was Box's duty to choose the arbitration board, but he angered the Simplot group by selecting the Box Energy Board of Directors.

No one was surprised when the board of arbitration and the jury came to different conclusions. After an investigation, the arbitration board agreed that Box, in his handling of the pipeline transaction, had violated his responsibilities to the shareholders and ordered him to give up 250,000 shares of company stock with a market value of $2.8 million (at just over $11 a share)—a much smaller amount than the $28 million awarded by the jury.

Simplot refused to accept the board's decision. The board, he said, was not independent at all but was made up of Box's cronies. The arbitrators could never be fair and impartial because each member sitting in judgment of Cloyce Box served at Box's pleasure. Many of them had longtime relationships with Box and at least one was currently doing business with him.

Box argued that his appointed board was honorable, independent, unbiased, and unprejudiced. The board, he said, conducted a "thorough investigation" of the situation and that he and the board reached a settlement that was "a product of hard-nosed negotiations."[16]

"Not so," said a spokesman for the Simplot group. "Mr. Box 'negotiated' this settlement with his hand-picked committee co-chairmen. The committee conducted an inadequate investigation which consisted of relying upon citations to the record and memoranda prepared by attorneys who represented Mr. Box at trial."[17]

In the end, Judge Maloney agreed with the Simplot group, and on December 20, 1993 (seven weeks after Cloyce Box died), Maloney entered the jury's verdict in the books. Box's estate owed OKC-LP shareholders $28 million.[18]

While the lawsuit dragged on, Cloyce Box used the time to shuffle his assets and shield his money as best he could. The trick he used was similar to the sale of the South Pass pipeline. It was a business sleight of hand that shifted money and stock through a confusing maze of interlocking companies that he owned or controlled. In this case, he pledged all his shares of Box Energy Corp. to Box Brothers Holding Company (owned by Box and his sons) as security against a $16 million loan.

When Cloyce died suddenly in 1993, Doug Box declared his father's estate in default on the loan and foreclosed. That meant that the Box Energy stock worth $43 million was transferred from Cloyce Box to Box Brothers Holding Co. to pay the $16 million loan.

Later, Box Brothers filed for bankruptcy in Delaware, in an attempt to put company stock out of reach of creditors. Since Cloyce Box was personally liable for the $28 million judgment, plus interest, the move temporarily shielded the money that could have been used to pay the debt.[19]

The cased dragged on for years. After Cloyce died, Don, Gary, and Doug Box wanted to end the incredibly expensive and time-consuming legal feud. They entered into negotiations to settle with Simplot. Tom Box wanted to keep fighting and split with his brothers. Soon, the Box brothers were suing each other over the future of Box Energy. The matter was finally settled at their mother's kitchen table, but the emotional damage never completely healed.

Then in August 1997, after one of the most intense court battles in the history of business, the Box brothers settled their legal feud with the Idaho potato king. US District Judge Joe Kendall approved the settlement that called for an end to all lawsuits involving the Box brothers and J. R. Simplot.

Simplot first reached agreement with Don, Gary, and Doug Box, and then a few weeks later came to terms with Tom. Under the agreement, Simplot acquired 57% of Box Energy Class A voting stock and 67% of Class B stock. The same agreement gave Simplot the right to purchase Cloyce Box's stock in CKB Petroleum—the company whose purchase of the pipeline touched off the legal battle.[20]

There was another side to Cloyce Box that didn't always square with the brazen and cold-hearted businessman.

"The press made Cloyce out to be dishonest and greedy," said Maurice Campbell, "but he wasn't that way at all. Don't make too much of all the lawsuits. It was common for big businesses to spend a lot of time in court. Guys would battle each other in court during the day and go to social events together at night. That's just the way

business was done. That was no reflection on Cloyce Box as a man. I've watched him be as aggressive as any businessman, but on a personal level, away from the boardroom, he could be the best friend you ever had."

"He was a sentimental man," Campbell said. "I've seen him be unusually kind to his employees. He had compassion for people less fortunate than he was, and that feeling was sincere. He helped a lot of people in quiet ways. He especially loved his old teammates in Detroit and would do anything for them."[21]

In 1982, Box organized a reunion to celebrate the thirtieth anniversary of the Lions' 1952 National Football League Championship season. The reunion was held in conjunction with Super Bowl XVI, played that year at the Silverdome in Pontiac, Michigan, just outside Detroit.

What a difference thirty years had made. In 1952, the results of the NFL Championship Game were buried deep in the sports pages in a few big city newspapers. By 1982, Super Bowl Sunday was practically a national holiday.

The 1982 reunion in Detroit was a happy occasion, but it had some sad and unintended consequences. When the old-timers arrived in Detroit, it was plain that some of them were not doing well. Box watched broken-hearted as some of his teammates limped into the room, their bodies broken from their years in the NFL.

Life wasn't so grand for some of the old guys. Many of them had bad backs, worn-out knees, and early-stage dementia, but no money for medical treatment. There was not yet a pension or benefits for players who retired before 1959. Some of the greatest players of all time lived in poverty when their playing days ended.

Many people felt sorry for the old guys, but Cloyce Box did something about it. That winter, he set aside 1 million dollars of his private funds to establish C. B. Trust, a Dallas-based charity for former NFL players who had fallen on hard times.

Trustees for C. B. Trust included Frank Gifford, Phyllis George, and Roger Staubach. Interest generated by the fund gave assistance to former NFL players who were having financial difficulties.

By 2000, the fund had paid out over $300,000 to help former NFL stars with utility bills, wheelchairs, and medical care. The fund even purchased a new set of tires for a former player who could not afford them.

When the trust was finally terminated in 2007 in accordance with New York state law, the trustees unanimously agreed to remit the remaining balance of $3,000 to the Jonesboro High School athletic department in memory of Cloyce Kennedy Box.

The fund was a well-kept secret to avoid the possible humiliation of the proud men it served. Few people knew of the fund's existence. Even Box's closest friends did not know of his generosity.

"I didn't know about the fund," said Box's friend and teammate Yale Lary, "but I knew he was a man who would never forget his buddies."[22]

Despite Box's efforts to keep the old-timer's fund a secret, some people around his old home in Jonesboro and Coryell County knew that one of the beneficiaries was the legendary lineman Bulldog Turner. "I was there the day he [Box] and Doak Walker and Bobby Layne met and agreed to start the old timers' fund," Maurice Campbell recalled. "Not long after that Cloyce went to Bulldog Turner's house near Gatesville and gave him a substantial sum of money. He did it quietly. He didn't want to embarrass anybody. He really cared about those old guys and didn't want them to suffer."[23]

Kentucky Governor John Y. Brown Jr. called Cloyce Box "a warm and caring person. He had that Hollywood look—soft eyes and great physique. But he had a humble nature. He never bragged on himself. And he really cared about his friends."

"I had a heart attack in Ft. Lauderdale one Fourth of July weekend. I knew something was wrong, but the EKG didn't show anything. The doctor went home. My wife Phyllis (George) was in LA with Cloyce and his wife. As soon as Cloyce found out what had happened, he came to get me. He flew across the country that night to get me out of there."[24]

Yale Lary described Box as "thoughtful and sensitive. He was a man's man, but he was kind-hearted and generous. No one ever had a better friend."[25]

"Cloyce Box was a generous man," David Ownby said, "and loyal to his friends. When I worked at OKC, Cloyce hired Rob Layne, Bobby Layne's son. No one was quite sure what Rob did, but Cloyce kept him on the payroll. I think Cloyce hired Rob out of loyalty to Bobby Layne."[26]

Writer and Newsweek *Bureau Chief, Hugh Aynesworth, said Box "had a strong personality but at the same time he was shy and almost humble. There was a soft side to him that not everyone saw."*

"Once I flew with him to Ecuador. We were there for three or four days. I didn't have much to do, so one morning I went to a park in Quito.

Walking along there, I saw an amazing sight—maybe twenty or thirty people who were disfigured in some way. I never saw anything like it. Why they were all together in one place I don't know."

"Later when I had lunch with Cloyce, I told him what I saw, and he insisted that we go back to the park together. When Cloyce saw the people I told him about, he spoke to each of them and gave them some money. Not a lot of money, but enough to show he cared about them. When he spoke to them, he was almost apologetic."

"When I looked at him, tears were streaming down his face."[27]

16

Bigger 'n Dallas

Contracts were made to be broken, honey,
but a handshake is the law of God.

—J. R. Ewing

Cloyce Box had always been a distant husband and father. He had reached a level of success in business that most men only dream of, but that success came at a price. He was busy running his companies and had little time for anniversaries, birthday parties, and little league baseball games. Fern was there for the boys, but Cloyce was often absent.

The virtues instilled in him as a boy in Jonesboro—a rigid mental toughness, an inability to admit mistakes, long hours of hard work, supreme confidence in his own judgment—made him a highly successful CEO, but were not characteristics of an ideal family man. At the office, he was the unchallenged leader with almost dictatorial powers, but effective leadership of a modern family requires more give and take.

Most boys learn to be good family men from their fathers, but Cloyce's role model wasn't around. He left the family when Cloyce was thirteen. A distant husband and father was all Cloyce knew how to be.

Cloyce Box was a brilliant businessman, but like the rest of us, a flawed human being. On a personal level, he could be warmhearted and generous with his time and money. His employees revered him. His friends admired and respected him. His mother and his sisters adored him. But he was not good at showing affection to those closest to him. He had time for everybody but his own wife and sons.

"My dad was very guarded about his feelings," Doug Box said. "He didn't share a lot of his personal matters with us. He never revealed much about himself. He was a tough father in many ways, and it was not always easy growing up in his house. He was gone a lot. He gave so much attention to his businesses. He wasn't the kind of father that was home at 5:30 every day. He was my father and I loved him, but I wasn't close to him. None of us were."[1]

The four Box sons went to the best schools and grew up with every advantage money could buy, but without a close relationship with the most important man in their lives. Don was the brilliant one—educated at the prestigious St. Marks School in Dallas, the University of Pennsylvania, and Wharton School of Business. Gary was the rebellious one. Tom was charismatic and athletic—the son most like Cloyce. Tom played football at Baylor and became a lawyer. Doug was artistic and sensitive—like his mother. He dabbled in music while a student at the University of Texas at Austin, much to his father's displeasure. Doug was the one who tried to keep peace when the brothers got crossways with each other.

While Cloyce mingled with the richest and most powerful people on earth, his relationship with Fern fell apart. A successful marriage requires hard work and commitment, but Cloyce was committed to other things. He neglected his most precious assets. He was an absentee father and an unfaithful husband.

"We knew there were problems between them," Doug Box said about his mother and father, "but they both kept quiet about it to protect us. In those days, a married couple stayed together for the good of the family. And they kept their feelings to themselves. But we knew."[2]

Pain is hard to hide, but Fern did her best. While battling loneliness and depression, she managed the household and held things together until the boys were grown. Then Phyllis George introduced Cloyce to her friend Ashley Scott Smith and even the pretense of propriety stopped.

Ashley was a 39-year-old beauty from a family of Louisiana social and political heavyweights. Her father, Nauman Steele Scott, was a prominent Louisiana attorney and a US District Judge appointed to the bench by Richard Nixon. Ashley's mother, Blanch Moulton Hammond Scott, was a reporter for the *New Orleans Times-Picayune* and a television reporter and talk show host on KALB-TV in Alexandria. Ashley's brother, Nauman Steele Scott III, was an oil and gas entrepreneur and president of Black Top Records—a New Orleans blues and rock label whose list of artists included the Neville Brothers, Maria Muldaur, W. C. Clark, and Omar and the Howlers. A second brother, John Wyeth "Jack" Scott was a New Orleans attorney, a college professor, and a three-term Louisiana congressman who cast the key vote that killed the Equal Rights Amendment in the Louisiana legislature. A third brother, Arthur Hammond Scott, was a founder of Black Top Records and Assistant District Attorney for New Orleans Parish.

Ashley was a beautiful woman who turned heads wherever she went. She was an interior designer, a socialite, and a former fashion model. In 1963, she married Junius Emmitt Smith, a wealthy Dallas furniture store executive, and still later, she would marry Byron McLean "Mack" Rankin in a stunning ceremony in Bali, Indonesia. Rankin worked for Hunt Oil and then as an independent operator with headquarters in New Orleans.

In 1982, Ashley Scott Smith served as the chairman of the Cattle Baron's Ball—an exclusive event for the Dallas social elite billed as the world's largest single-night fund-raiser for cancer research. Everybody who was anybody in Dallas came to the ball dressed in his or her gaudiest and most expensive western attire. Only the crème de la crème of Dallas society was invited and only the movers and shakers of the highest order were asked to host.

Cloyce and Fern hosted the 1982 Cattle Baron's Ball at the Box Ranch in Frisco. The theme for the night was "A Wild West Evening Under the Stars." Dallas couples, dressed in silver buckles, Stetson hats, and alligator boots, danced through the night to the music of Willie Nelson and his band. The event raised $300,000 for cancer research.

Ashley and Cloyce spent a lot of time together planning the event. By the time Willie Nelson launched into "Whiskey River" that night at Box Ranch, Cloyce and Ashley were in love.

At the time their relationship began, Cloyce and Ashley were each married to someone else, but they made little effort to keep their affair a secret. When Fern could take no more, she sued for divorce ending a roller-coaster ride that began thirty-seven years earlier in business law class.[3]

The affair played out in the background of an all-out business feud between two wealthy families (Box and Adams) over controlling interest in a Texas oil company (OKC Corp.). Each side accused the other of shady deals and dirty business practices in connection with the friendly brokers. Both families were heavily involved in cattle and oil. The two families were once close, but their relationship turned hostile in a bitter fight over power and money.

The patriarch of one family was the CEO and chairman of the board of the disputed oil company. He was egocentric and manipulative. He was unhappily married to a Texas beauty and had eyes for another. His mother was a strong-willed countrywoman of humble origin who instilled a fierce pride in her ambitious son. Until her death, she was the only person to whom her son would listen.

If the whole affair sounds like an episode from the TV show "Dallas," in a way it was.

When Cloyce and Fern first moved to Dallas, they bought a house at 4241 Park Lane. When the family outgrew that place, Box bought 300 acres near Allen. The place was really a farm, but Cloyce transformed it into a cutting horse ranch. Farming did not fit his image. As a child in Jonesboro, he learned that poor folks farmed, but rich folks ranched.

Then in 1967, Box paid $250,000 for the ranch in Frisco. At the time, the ranch house was little more than the biggest dwelling in a sleepy little town, but in a few years the house would become, for a brief time, the most famous domicile in America next to the big white house at 1600 Pennsylvania Avenue.

Box raised the money to buy the house and surrounding property in Frisco from an illegal insider stock deal. In 1966, a stockbroker approached Box with inside information about a company soon to receive approval from the Food and Drug Administration for its version of a product that would change the world: the birth control pill. The general market would not receive the news for quite a while. Box borrowed as much money as he could, bought all the stock he could afford, and later sold the stock for a $250,000 profit. He used the money to buy the Frisco property. In 1974, he bought 495 adjoining acres for $2.7 million.

"My father loved that ranch," said Doug Box. "In a way, it was a return to his country roots. He was a cowboy at heart. He loved cattle, and he loved horses. He wanted to run the ranch himself, but he had no time. He needed a good ranch foreman, but wasn't happy with anybody for long. He was picky, demanding, and hard to work for. He hired dozens of ranch foremen but fired them all. Nobody could please him."[4]

Box bought the ranch and the house that went with it for $3 million, and then made improvements that dramatically increased its value. In 1983, when Box needed money to build a cement plant in Midlothian, he mortgaged the entire property to an insurance company for $75 million. That decision proved to be a tragic mistake, but at the time, Trammell Crow called it the greatest real estate deal he had ever seen.

When Box bought the property it was rundown, but he hired craftsmen who turned it into a showplace. There was a 25,000-square-foot indoor riding arena, a staffed veterinary hospital, a five-car garage, and an 11,000-square-foot tractor barn. The horse barns were immaculate—kept like a marine barracks. Box insisted that saddles and bridles be hung up in a certain way and every tool stored in its proper location. If he found something out of place, the culprit had hell to pay.

The main ranch house was bigger than a Super Walmart. It was a neighborhood conversation piece, but few people outside the small town of Frisco knew anything about it. Then one day in 1980, Doug Box, at the time a student at the University of Texas at Austin, called home and got some very interesting news.

"My mom answered the phone," he recalled. "We talked a few minutes and then she said 'By the way there's a camera crew here to film a television show.' She told me it was a soap opera for nighttime television. We all thought it was a dumb idea—no one would watch it. Boy, were we wrong. The popularity of the show took us all by surprise."[5]

Soon, television watchers around the world were familiar with the Box Ranch house at the corner of FM 720 and Preston Road in

Frisco, as the first home of the Ewings from the television show "Dallas."

Architect John Astin Perkins designed and built the house in 1941 as a replica of Tara from the film *Gone with the Wind*. It was a colossal, rambling, antebellum-style mansion with twenty-eight rooms and a full basement.

It held more treasures than King Solomon's temple. Box filled the house with lavish furnishings including antique crystal chandeliers, a priceless collection of western art, and two French fireplace mantels, one rumored to have belonged to Napoleon. Film crews used the house for the exterior shots of the fictional Southfork Ranch in the first five episodes of "Dallas."

Cloyce Box, whose personal life and business methods bore an uncanny resemblance to the fictional J. R. Ewing, was a part of the show from the very beginning. In fact, the idea of a television show about Dallas got its start with Box and a former Dallas mayor who wanted to clean up the city's image.

"The Mayor of Dallas at the time was a man named Bobby Folsom," Tom Box explained. "Bobby and my father were good friends. The two of them talked about ways to promote Dallas. At the time, Dallas did not have a good image. The city was known as the place where an American president was murdered. So dad, Bobby, and some other people who cared about Dallas got together to discuss ways to improve the city's image. One idea that surfaced was a television show about Dallas. That's where it all started."

"A television production company in California called Lorimar got interested in the project, so the city of Dallas flew some of the Lorimar guys out here to look around. They scouted several locations, but when they saw our house in Frisco, they wanted to shoot the TV show there."

"My father wasn't interested. This was our home, and my mother and father wanted to keep it a quiet place. But the Lorimar guys wanted to use our house, so Bobby Folsom asked my father to allow the show to be filmed at our house as a personal favor. My father said yes, but he wasn't too happy about it. He was reluctant to get involved in the television show. That wasn't his style."

Tom Box recalled when he first heard that his house was about to become the set for a television show. "One night at the dinner table, my father made a grand announcement. He told us boys that a company was going to film a television show at our house. He also said the producers wanted to use one of us as an extra in the show. So my father went around the table and asked each of us if we wanted to be on television. Each of us said no, which was what my father wanted us to say. 'Good,' my father said. 'cause that's what I already told 'em.' I think that illustrates my father's feelings about the situation. He wasn't excited about it at all."

"Still, everyone involved in the project was great to us. All the actors and actresses—we knew them well. Larry Hagman and Barbara Bel Geddes went out of their way to talk with us. And we were all completely surprised by the popularity of the show. No one believed it would take off like it did."[6]

The Box Ranch had always been a quiet place, but as soon as the television crew arrived, tranquility and privacy ceased to exist. A fleet of 18-wheelers rolled through the gate carrying all kinds of heavy equipment. There were forty to sixty people, not counting the actors and actresses, who worked twelve hours a day, six days a week. There was an array of make-up artists, hairdressers, grips, extras, food service people, and security.

The premise of the show seemed preposterous to many Texans. Dallas, after all, was the least Texan of all the Texas cities. There were few cattle in Dallas County and not a drop of oil. The evil villain of the show was the real-life son of Weatherford's own Mary Martin who played Peter Pan on Broadway.

Even the filming of the show began in an un-Texas-like fashion. A rare snowstorm interrupted the first day of shooting at the Box Ranch.

The Dallas media hated the show and lambasted it on every occasion. Many Dallasites couldn't shake the feeling that the whole thing was an inside joke—that Hollywood was making fun of them.

Dallas quietly debuted on April 2, 1978, as a five-part miniseries on CBS. There were no plans for more episodes. But the show, a crazy combination of *Romeo and Juliet*, *Cain and Abel*, *Giant*, and *The Young and the Restless*, caught on and became a huge hit in the

United States and around the world. It became one of the longest lasting prime-time dramas in American television history—lasting fourteen seasons. Only *Bonanza, Law and Order*, and *Gunsmoke* had longer runs.

A staggering 83 million viewers tuned in to see who shot J. R. in November 1980—at the time the highest-rated episode in the history of television. *Dallas* won four Emmys. It was translated and dubbed into sixty-seven languages in ninety countries. J. R. Ewing's Stetson is in the Smithsonian.

Despite Box's misgivings, the relationship between Texas and Hollywood was smooth as bourbon and branch water—for a time.

"When I signed," Linda Gray (Sue Ellen) recalled, "the arrangement was that we would shoot the pilot in Texas, but the rest of the show would be shot here (California). But things worked out well in Texas, and the ranch we were using was established in the filming so they decided to go back there and do the whole show there." Cloyce Box did everything he could to make it work. In one scene, Sue Ellen rode up on horseback astride an animal from the show's regular string. "But Cloyce said it didn't look good enough for me," She recalled. "So he had one of his hands bring out one of his own horses—a $60,000 gelding."[7]

"In the beginning, the whole thing was exciting for us boys" Tom Box remembered, "but in the long haul, it was no picnic having a popular television series filmed at your house. It just didn't fit. My mother and father couldn't stand it. The whole thing started with a small idea. There were no great expectations. It was done as a favor. But for us, it was a complete disaster. Before the show, our house was a quiet place—off the beaten path. After the show debuted, people showed up at our house at all hours of the day and night. They would literally walk into our house looking for Larry Hagman. They walked all over our property. They left trash. They stole bricks and left the gates open. The horses got out."[8]

There were also reports that the storyline went in directions that were unsatisfactory to the real oil tycoon who owned the real Southfork. Cloyce Box was particularly unhappy with the racy nature of the show and the callous and greedy depiction of freewheeling oilmen who spent their time cheating and suing each other by day and drinking together by night. The show, after all, was supposed to be fiction.

But the worst part for Cloyce Box was that the wild popularity of the show brought busloads of tourists who wandered all over the property and disturbed the tranquility of his home place. After five episodes, Box booted the television crews.

In a panic, the producer went on the hunt for another Southfork. He found one in the 4,769-square-foot ranch house on Duncan Acres in Plano.

"Dallas" was a huge success, and it accomplished its more serious purpose. It showcased the city and polished its image. People in remote corners of the world recognized the Dallas skyline, and tourists flocked to J. R.'s hometown to visit the landmarks made popular by the show. They made pilgrimages to the Box Ranch in Frisco and to Duncan Acres. They took pictures standing in front of the fictional Ewing Oil building, which was really Bryan Tower—Trammell Crow's forty-story office building at 2001 Bryan Street in downtown Dallas. Ewing Oil later moved to offices in the fifty-six-story Renaissance Tower at 1201 Elm Street.

Just how much the lives of Cloyce Box, J. R. Simplot, Boots Adams, Oscar Wyatt, and Trammel Crow inspired the storyline and the characters for *Dallas* is debatable, but the parallels are unmistakable. Although the show's credits claimed that any similarity to real people was purely coincidental, no one could deny that there were plenty of real-life Texas characters around to fuel the imaginations of Hollywood screenwriters.

Box's friend David Ownby suggested that the name "J. R." came from J. R. Adams of Guymon, Oklahoma, one of Box's horseracing friends and one of OKC's friendly brokers. It may only be coincidence that the wife of Ashburn Bywaters, one of Box's early business associates, was Barbara Ewing.

Although the fictional Ewings were promiscuously entertaining, they couldn't hold a candle to the scheming, the conniving, the backstabbing, and the intrigue of the real-life characters whose philandering, infidelity, and shady business deals turned family members against one another and caused old friendships to crumble like burned toast.

"The Ewings were shadows of people we knew who were far more despicable and greedy," said Tom Box.[9]

The real J. R. Ewing agreed. "I know the dudes down here," said Larry Hagman, a real-live Texan from Weatherford. "If we did the real Dallas, they wouldn't let it on the air."[10]

In 1984, the Southland Corporation chose the Box Ranch to host a reception for Mary Lou Retton, Greg Louganis, and the entire US Olympic Team. There were fireworks in the shape of the US flag and Olympic symbols floating in the swimming pool. That night, 10,000 people roamed the house and the property. Guests included Boz Scaggs and Darrell Royal.

In 1992, the city of Dallas hosted the Ambassador's Forum—a meeting of ambassadors and consular officials from around the world. It was a chance to showcase the new Dallas as a world-class city—an Athens on the Plains.

In conjunction with that event, Cloyce and Ashley (they married in 1986) threw a grand celebration at the Frisco ranch for the ambassadors and a few select friends including Ron Haddock, CEO of Fina; country singers Charley Pride and Rudy Gatlin; world champion cowboy Larry Mahan; Randy White and Bill Bates of the Dallas Cowboys; Caroline Rose Hunt, daughter of legendary oilman H. L. Hunt; Tess Harper, the actress who starred with Robert Duvall in the film Tender Mercies *shot in Palmer just south of Dallas; and the Academy Award-winning actor Jack Palance. But the real star of the show was Russian Ambassador Vladimir Lukin who earned the nickname "Vladi-Bob" after getting tanked up on vodka and Lone Star Beer and riding Box's stuffed bull.*

The party ran late into the night. When the bar ran low on beer, volunteers hopped in their limos and drove to the Fina Station down the street to reload. The next night, the party continued in the main ballroom at Trammell Crow's Loews Anatole Hotel.[11]

17

The Fate of All Dreamers

Invest in seven ventures, yes, in eight; you do not know what disaster may come upon the land.

—Ecclesiastes 11:2

In July 1993, Cloyce Box chartered a Gulfstream G-4 jet to take his family on a 2-week vacation to Europe. At sixty-nine, he was the oldest pilot certified by Gulfstream to fly a G-4. In the coming weeks, he would fly to business meetings all over the southwest and to Frank Gifford's book release party in New York City.

On September 4, 1993, Ashley threw a 70th birthday party for Cloyce at their home in Dallas. Carol Layne was there. So were former Lion's teammates Fred Enke Jr., Yale Lary, and Harley Sewell. Other guests included the horse trainer J. J. Pletcher, Blake Turner of the New York Jets, and Frank Cannon—Box's business partner from Belton.

Box still had a great presence for a man who just turned 70, but his once magnificent body was beginning to show its age. His hair was thinning, and he had lost some weight, sharpening the features of his face. Only his family knew that he had early stage Parkinson's disease, and for several years he had been under the care of a North Carolina cardiologist for an inverted T wave and an irregular heartbeat. The family was concerned, but only Cloyce and his doctor knew how far his heart disease had progressed.

Of more immediate concern for Box was a series of business difficulties that threatened to destroy everything he had built. He was a private man who always tried to keep his troubles to himself, but secrets were getting harder to keep.

"Cloyce Box was a talented businessman," his friend Maurice Campbell recalled, "but he was a risk-taker. That was his strength and his downfall. He made a couple of disastrous decisions in his life that turned out to be tragic mistakes. One was the refusal to settle with J. R. Simplot. That court battle drained a lot of his resources. But the biggest mistake was to build the cement plant in Midlothian."[1]

The town of Midlothian, located thirty miles south of Dallas, is the hub of the cement industry in North Texas. A geological formation called the Austin Chalk Escarpment runs north and south through town, and that formation is rich in limestone and clay—the ingredients for making cement. Today, there are eleven cement plants in Texas. Three are in the Cement Valley of Midlothian.

The city calls itself the Cement Capital of Texas. Midlothian has more cement plants and more kilns (eight) than any other city in the United States.

While all seems well in Midlothian, there is an undercurrent of apprehension between the residents and the cement plants that rears its head from time to time. The townspeople understand that cement brings economic prosperity. It is a necessary ingredient in a healthy, robust economy. The plants in Midlothian provide good-paying jobs, and the taxes they generate pay for city parks, modern school buildings, football stadiums, and teacher salaries.

But there has always been a lingering fear that the stuff coming out of the smokestacks is unhealthy. The people of Midlothian sometimes wonder if the prosperity the plants bring is worth the potential risks to their health and the health of their children.

In 1985, Cloyce Box and Trammell Crow built a $91 million cement plant 2.5 miles northeast of Midlothian, on Highway 67 in Ellis County. At the time, the plant was one of the largest in the world, capable of producing 1 million tons of cement annually. Box and Crow built the facility to meet Texas Air Control Board and US Environmental Protection Agency standards. The plant was licensed to use coal or natural gas to fire its kiln.

Box had hoped to build the plant almost entirely with public money, but his company, OKC-LP, was chartered strictly as an oil company, limiting its ability to raise funds outside its defined purpose. So the money to build the facility came from $40.5 million in private equity, a large bank loan, and $27.6 million in bonds issued by the state of Texas. The city of Midlothian was the overseer of the bonds.

Cloyce Box and Trammell Crow each owned 50% of the company, but (and this fact would prove crucial) Box had to guarantee everything including whatever losses Crow might incur. Box had to agree to that stipulation for Crow to sign on.[2]

Still, Box had great expectations for the Midlothian cement plant. He envisioned the facility would provide cement for the great North Texas building boom that was turning empty prairie land into an endless suburbia. Box once made a fortune in the cement business in Oklahoma, and he believed he could do it again in North Texas. The kiln was fired in 1987.

The project seemed like a sure thing, but the cement business had grown more complicated since the old days when Box got rich making cement in Pryor, Oklahoma. For one thing, cement was now an international business and much more competitive than it used to be.

In 1986, the United States, Canada, and Mexico began negotiations to eliminate barriers to trade on the North American continent. The talks would eventually lead to the North American Free Trade Agreement (NAFTA) in 1994, but soon after the talks began, all kinds of products began moving freely across the US border.

With trade restrictions beginning to ease, the huge Mexican cement company, Cemex, made a play to grab a share of the American market. In the late 1980s, the company began selling a gray Portland cement in the United States at less than market value.[3] This kind of business strategy, called "dumping," is an example of predatory pricing, especially in the context of international trade. Dumping is not technically illegal, but it can do great harm to domestic producers, especially those companies not on firm financial ground.

The Box-Crow plant was heavily in debt and depended on a healthy cash flow to pay its creditors. The dumping of Mexican cement on the American market, along with a slump in construction, drew significant business away from Box-Crow and cut deeply into its profits. Publically, the ownership showed optimism, but

Cloyce Box could read a balance sheet. Privately, he knew that income was falling short of expenses. The plant was in trouble from the beginning.

At the same time the Box-Crow plant experienced declining demand for its product, the industry came under siege from environmentalists. Cement plants had a history of emitting carbon dioxide, heavy metals, and poisonous dust and gases into the atmosphere. There was concern that emissions from the Midlothian plants were poisoning the air and ground water.

At first, the people in Midlothian with worries about emissions were isolated and unorganized. They had concerns, especially about a strong sulfur-like smell and a trail of dead vegetation downwind from the plants.

Then, just as concern was building, word leaked to the public that the TXI plant in Midlothian, in an effort to reduce costs, was seeking a permit from the federal government to burn hazardous waste in its kilns. When local residents—already jittery about poisonous emissions—heard the news, they rose in opposition.

Because extremely high temperatures are required to bring about the reactions necessary to produce clinker (2,700 to 3,000 degrees Fahrenheit), the process of manufacturing cement is energy intensive. Energy costs account for 40% of the total cost of manufacturing cement. Some kilns burn up to 12 tons of coal per hour. If cement plants could supplement expensive natural gas and coal with a cheaper alternative, like waste-derived fuel, the plants could save millions in operating expenses.

In the beginning, the federal government saw the burning of hazardous wastes in cement plants as killing two birds with one stone. Each year, American industry produced millions of tons of petrochemical by-products, used motor oil, old tires, paint thinner, cleaning solutions, and solvents. The stuff was too toxic to put in landfills, so burning it in high-temperature kilns seemed like a good way to get rid of it. And cement companies jumped at the chance to save millions in energy costs. Not only was the fuel free, the plants were paid to burn it.

But public opinion is a powerful and unpredictable force, and when government regulators granted TXI a permit to burn hazardous wastes in its kilns in lieu of coal or natural gas, there were protests and public hearings. When the Gifford-Hill North Texas Cement Plant, also in Midlothian, began burning hazardous wastes in its kilns, the small pockets of concerned citizens, aroused by sensational stories in the print and electronic media, grew and coalesced into a single voice of opposition.[4]

Despite reports from several government agencies that emission levels of the plants burning wastes were within acceptable limits, there were protests and angry town meetings. People feared carcinogens in the air and the decline of property values. Despite government reports to the contrary, there were rumors of increased levels of mercury, cadmium, and hydrogen sulfide in the air, soil, and water.

Local citizens opposed to the burning of hazardous wastes formed CAUSE (Citizens Aware and United for a Safe Environment) and Downwinders at Risk. One group with a sense of humor called itself CACA (Cleaner Air through Citizen Action).

Then the Sierra Club got involved, and all three Midlothian plants came under the close scrutiny of a state government agency called the Texas Natural Resource Conservation Commission (TNRCC). Officials at the TNRRC stated publicly that they intended to crack down on the practice of burning hazardous wastes at cement plants and began a campaign to compel plants to reduce emissions. The agency imposed strict new regulations on all cement plants in Texas.

The problem for Box-Crow was that the expense of meeting those regulations drove up operating costs just as cheap cement from Mexico, dumped on the American market, cut into profits. The Box-Crow plant could not generate enough income to repay its loans.

In 1989, a group of domestic cement producers, including Box-Crow, filed an antidumping petition with the US Department of Commerce alleging that the dumping of gray Portland cement and clinker from Mexico was causing injury to the American cement industry. The group claimed that the price charged in the United States for Mexican cement was about half what was charged in Mexico.[5]

Box hoped that the petition would force the Department of Commerce to come to the aid of the domestic cement industry, but the government moves at a snail's pace. As officials studied the matter, the Box-Crow plant continued to bleed money.

Box tried to borrow funds to cover expenses, but banking had changed from the old days when he could borrow millions with a phone call. In the 1980s, a new state law allowed Texas banks for the first time to consolidate with banks from other states. Suddenly, many of the biggest banks in Dallas, once controlled by Box's circle of friends, sold out to tough bankers from North Carolina, Ohio, and New York.

Cloyce Box did not have a personal relationship with the new generation of out-of-state bankers. He was unable to use the power of his personality because he had difficulty arranging face-to-face meetings with the new guys. They were more interested in balance sheets and bottom lines than in friendships. The good old boys were no longer in charge.

Elaborate contingency plans and extensive exit strategies had always been hallmarks of Box's business arrangements, and he was famous for manipulating people and situations to get the outcomes he wanted. He had always been diversified enough to weather a financial storm, and since the George A. Fuller sale he always had safeguards to protect his private assets. But this time, things went horribly wrong.

Looking back, it is clear that Box was taken down in part by overconfidence. After the successful court fight with the Securities and Exchange Commission, Box believed he was unstoppable. Furthermore, he believed the Midlothian Cement Plant was a sure thing. He never dreamed it would fail. Thirty years earlier, the cement business made him wealthy, and there was no reason to believe this time would be any different. But it was different.

It is likely that a part of Box's plan was to manage the risk of the cement plant with income from the transport fees from his Louisiana pipeline, but J. R. Simplot had the pipeline bottled up in court, draining Box's resources, and casting doubt on the legality of the whole deal.

Box had faced financial difficulties before, but this time he was particularly vulnerable. He had nothing in reserve. He was all in. It was sink or swim, and he was sinking fast.

Desperate for money, he went to Trammell Crow's office at 2100 McKinney Avenue in Dallas. He needed a financial transfusion from his partner to save the Midlothian Cement Plant. By then, he was mortgaged to the hilt and had nowhere else to turn. He hoped that Crow would agree to pump enough cash into the project to hold creditors at bay until the dispute over Mexican cement could be resolved and construction picked up.

Box and Crow had been through a lot together. They were friends and partners. In the old days, they shared a hotel room in New York to save money. Crow never forgot that Box saved him by convincing Northrup to take Fuller off their hands. Crow had always come through in the past, and Box was hopeful that this time would be no different.

But at the moment, Crow had bigger problems that an unprofitable cement plant.

In the late 1980s, the American economy took a nosedive. First, there was a savings and loan (S&L) crisis that led to the failure of over 700 S&L institutions along with the Federal Savings and Loan Insurance Corporation, the organization established to insure S&L deposits. The book value of the bankrupt S&Ls was over $400 billion. The shaky economy teetered on the edge of the abyss.

Then on October 17, 1987 (Black Monday), panicky investors began selling their stocks. The collapse began in Hong Kong and spread to Europe. The Dow Jones fell 22% in a few hours. The world economy was in recession.

The Trammell Crow Company faced the worst real estate crash of modern times. To make matters worse, Crow had overbuilt, and he took a beating for it.[6] Many of his commercial properties sat vacant, while his real estate business suffered from declining values and a general tightening of credit. He closed twenty of his ninety offices worldwide and cut his employee workforce by a third.[7]

The year 1988 was especially bad. For every $1 in assets, the company owed 93 cents to creditors.

Although the Midlothian Cement Plant was one of the most expensive of its kind in the world, it was small potatoes compared to Crow's vast real estate empire. Facing a far greater disaster than the loss of a cement plant, Crow naturally turned his full attention to saving his real estate business. If something had to be sacrificed, it would be Midlothian Cement and his long friendship with Cloyce Box.

"It was a bad time for everybody," Doug Box explained. "A recession hit in 1987. Construction was flat. Demand for cement was down. There was a savings and loan crisis and bank failures. Our own bank failed."[8]

Another factor was a fundamental change in the Trammell Crow Company. Trammell had recently stepped aside to allow his son Harlan to run the organization. Cloyce Box did not have the long, intimate relationship with Harlan that he had with Trammell. And Harlan was trying to save the company. In the process, he stared down lenders and jettisoned some of his father's closest associates.

That day, Box suffered the fate of all dreamers. He left Crow's office disillusioned and empty-handed.

"Cloyce never said much, he was so secretive about his business," Maurice Campbell said, "but he was disappointed with Trammell Crow. Cloyce believed Trammell could have bailed him out but he didn't. Cloyce felt like Trammell let him down."[9]

A younger man could have rebounded. Trammell Crow had returned from the brink of disaster on several occasions—once with Box's help. But Box was too old to start over, and his health was worse than anyone knew.

While Box battled to save his empire, the Box-Crow plant fell behind in its payments. There was a glimmer of hope in 1989 when Box secured a $30 million working loan from Holnam Inc.—a global building materials and aggregate company controlled by Holder Bank, a Swiss company that owned numerous cement plants around the world. He hoped the money would allow his company to hold on until the dispute with Mexico could be settled and construction picked up.

But Box had to put his share of Box-Crow as collateral for the loan, and when cash flow problems and weak sales at Box-Crow persisted, the Swiss investors lost faith in Box-Crow's ability to make money. Believing it unlikely that Box-Crow could make its payments, Holnam called in the loan, throwing Box-Crow into bankruptcy in August 1992.

According to bankruptcy documents, Box-Crow Cement had assets of $141.19 million and liabilities of $190.4 million.[10]

Even Cloyce Box had to admit that he was beaten. J. R. Simplot had Box Energy tied up in court while the Box-Crow cement plant was unable to turn a profit. Box owed millions of dollars with no hope of paying his loans. At Box's request, the Midlothian City Council voted to transfer the state bonds from Box-Crow to Holnam.[11]

Financial difficulties put a strain on old friendships. In the bankruptcy process, Trammell Crow filed suit against Box, and Box sued one of the banks that financed the project.[12]

And bankruptcy was a double whammy for Box. Not only did he lose his own contribution to the deal, he had to guarantee Trammell Crow's losses.

Then in May 1993 Holnam, renamed Holcim, bought the Box-Crow plant, two distribution terminals, a quarry, and all working capital for pennies on the dollar and began operating the business as a wholly owned subsidiary. The fine print showed that Holcim had a partner in the deal. The partner was none other than Trammell Crow.[13]

"My father actually put up all the money for the Box-Crow cement plant," Doug Box explained. "Trammell didn't invest any money in the project, but he put up his signature property, the Village Apartments in Dallas, as collateral for an $18 million loan. Dad really wanted to do the project on his own, but he needed Trammell. Financially, dad couldn't do it all himself. The project was too big."

"Trammell didn't really want to do it. He didn't know anything about cement. He only did it as a favor to my dad. Trammell was really a surrogate partner."

"I have a picture of Dad and Trammell signing the papers to build Box-Crow. Dad was excited, but Trammell was troubled. You could see it in his face. He had doubts and was reluctant to get involved. He wasn't sure a cement plant was a good idea."

"When Box-Crow went bankrupt, Dad lost $40 million on the deal," Doug added. "It devastated our family. But, Trammell was a smooth talker and the master negotiator. In the Chapter 11 proceedings, he got his Village Apartments property released, and he winds up owning 25% of the company (Holcim). (The Schmidheiny family of Switzerland owns the other 75%.) Trammell made out like a bandit."

"But when Holcim put Box-Crow into bankruptcy, it wiped us out. The bankruptcy, combined with the money we spent on the Simplot deal took everything."[14]

The bankruptcy of Box-Crow placed a strain on a once great friendship. When the Midlothian deal went sour, Cloyce Box and Trammell Crow, once the best of friends who trusted each other with their fortunes, never spoke to each other again.

In the months that followed, the family learned the shocking news that Cloyce Box had pledged between 85 and 90% of his liquid net worth, including the Box ranches in Frisco, Ocala, and Moody, to secure financing for the Box-Crow Cement Plant. When Box-Crow folded, and the banks foreclosed, Box's estate was insolvent.

With a $1 million a year salary as CEO of Box Energy, Cloyce was able to keep up appearances for a time. It was only after his death that his empire completely collapsed. Creditors swooped in. The lien holder on his loans confiscated the Box ranches and sold them to satisfy a part of the debt.

According to the accounting firm of Coopers and Lybrand, Box's net worth in 1984 was $145,870,000 (about $350 million in 2014 dollars). At the time, he controlled one public company and eight private companies. He owned three ranches, three airplanes, a New York townhouse, a herd of cattle, and 200 horses.

In 1993, after the Box-Crow Cement Plant went bankrupt, Box's property was gone, and his estate was $85 million in the red.[15]

On October 24, 1993, Cloyce and Ashley boarded his twin-engine Beechcraft King Air at Addison Airport for a flight to Durham, North Carolina. Cloyce had an appointment with his cardiologist the next morning for his annual physical and cardiac stress test at Duke University Medical Center. That night, he and Ashley checked into the Sheraton Imperial Hotel on Emperor Avenue near the Duke University Campus. Box wasn't feeling well and went to bed early.

At 10 p.m., Cloyce Box suffered a massive heart attack and died in his bed.

Once a poor boy was born with remarkable talents. Like Solomon, he had great wisdom, strength, and vitality. Even at night his mind did not rest.

When he became a man, he undertook enormous projects. He accomplished great things and was proud of himself for all he had done. He had big dreams and made them come true. He built great structures. He lived in mansions and owned large herds. He amassed huge quantities of gold and silver, equal to the treasures of kings and provinces.

But the things of earth are temporary. Life is a cycle that eventually returns us all to the place where we started. It is the ability to enjoy life and be happy in our work that is the gift of God. All else is meaningless.

Like chasing the wind.

Notes

Chapter 1

1. Wilmuth Box-Johnson, letter to her family.
2. Ibid.
3. William S. Pugsley, *Imprint on the Land: Life Before Camp Hood, 1820–1942* (Austin, TX: Prewitt & Associations, 2001), 131.
4. Hayden Young, interview by author, June 22, 2008.

Chapter 2

1. Pugsley, *Imprint on the Land*, 138.
2. L. Louise Box, interview by the author, October 31, 2012.
3. Maurice Campbell, interview by the author, March 20, 2009.
4. Tom Box, interview by the author, June 8, 2012.
5. Wilmuth Box-Johnson, letter.
6. L. Louise Box, interview.
7. Wilmuth Box-Johnson, letter.
8. L. Louise Box, interview.
9. Wilmuth Box-Johnson, letter.
10. L. Louise Box, interview.
11. Wilmuth Box-Johnson, letter.
12. Tom Box, interview, June 8, 2012.
13. Maurice Campbell, interview, March 20, 2009.
14. L. Louise Box, interview.

Chapter 3

1. "Former Students Say 'Thanks' to Mr. and Mrs. Lemmons," *The Hamilton Herald-News*, June 1, 1972. When Mr. Lemmons retired as Jonesboro superintendent in 1972, Boyce Box gave P. T., Bess, and their son Tom a 15-day trip to Hawaii. "Lemmons Family Has Christmas in Hawaii," *The Hamilton Herald-News*, January 4, 1973.
2. Maurice Campbell, interview, March 20, 2009.
3. "Sports: Frank A. Godsoe,"*Amarillo Daily News*, April 23, 1965.
4. L. Louise Box, interview.
5. Doug Box, interview by the author, August 5, 2013.
6. Wilmuth Box-Johnson, letter.
7. "Giraffes in West Texas," *Time Magazine*, February 16, 1942.
8. "Baggett 'Spreading It On Thick' at NY," *Lubbock Morning Avalanche*, January 20, 1942.

9. Chick Halbert, from House, New Mexico, was reported to be the tallest basketball player in America. Before Halbert's arrival at West Texas State, the tallest man on campus was a 6'9" basketball player named Shackleford. When Halbert, officially 6'9 ¾", walked into Burton Gym, Shackleford was known forever after as "Shorty."

Halbert was unstoppable anytime he planted his size fifteen high tops low in the paint. His favorite shot when he got the ball close to his own goal was to face the rim, jump straight up in the air, and stuff the ball in the basket with both hands. Sportswriters did not know what to call such a shot. Only later was it called a slam dunk.

Unlike some tall basketball players, Halbert was not thin or fragile. He weighed 225 pounds and was muscular and tough. He had a rock-hard elbow and was not afraid to use it.

In the 1941 NAIA tournament, the Buffaloes played San Diego State, matching Halbert against the Aztec's 6'8" center Andy Echle. On the second trip down the court, Echle and Halbert tangled over a rebound. Halbert came down with the ball, while Echle hit the court with the back of his head and had to be assisted to the dressing room.

Even without their big man, the Aztecs, led by little All-American sharpshooter Milky Phelps, upset the Buffaloes 43-40 and went on to win the NAIA championship.

Halbert tried to enlist in the army during the World War II, but his height exceeded army regulations. In lieu of military service, he built airplanes for Boeing in Kansas and played Amateur Athletic Union basketball for the famed Phillips 66ers of Bartlesville, Oklahoma.

After the war, he played professionally for the Chicago Stags of the Basketball Association of America. (In 1949, the Basketball Association of America [BAA] merged with the National Basketball League to form the National Basketball Association, or the NBA.) His second year he was second team all-league. In 1947, the Stags sold Halbert's contract to the Philadelphia Warriors in a straight cash deal for $7,500, one of the highest prices ever paid for a basketball player at that time. He had his best year in 1947 when he scored 421 points and had 30 assists with the Warriors.

Later, Halbert played for the Boston Celtics, the Providence Steamrollers, the Washington Capitals, and the Baltimore Bullets. In his professional career, he averaged 8.8 points and 7.9 rebounds.

He remained a scrapper to the end of his career. In 1950, while playing for the Washington Capitals, the league warned him twice for rough play and fined him the astronomical sum of $100 for "unbecoming conduct."

In three years at Canyon, Price Brookfield scored almost 1,400 points, averaging just under 20 a game. On January 15, 1942, he scored 44 points against New Mexico State—a record that stood for decades.

At 6'4" and 190 pounds, Brookfield was a bruiser who could clear the lane when he went to the basket, but at the same time, he had a delicate one-handed set shot with either hand. He was a consensus All American in 1942 and the big man on campus when the Box twins first arrived in Canyon.

Brookfield served in the Navy during World War II, and then played his final season of college eligibility at Iowa State. After college, he played for several short-lived professional teams before professional basketball crystallized into a single major organization. He played for the American Gears of Chicago, the Butler All-Stars of Indiana, the Anderson Packers, and the Muncie Brammers of the Indiana Professional Basketball League, as well as in 61 games for the Indianapolis Jets and the Rochester Royals of the NBA. After his playing days ended, Brookfield coached high school basketball at McKinney, Texas.

Jack Maddox was born on a ranch near Quanah, Texas, and went to high school in Wichita Falls, Texas. He went to Southern Methodist University on a football scholarship but felt out of place in Dallas and dropped out. Then Al Baggett turned on the charm and recruited Maddox to play basketball at West Texas State—a small town environment that suited Maddox just fine. He was a 6'3" forward whose deadly shots from the perimeter fit perfectly with the power game of Price Brookfield and the post play of Charles Halbert.

Maddox was a little All American in 1941. He joined the Marines during World War II and played all over the world with an elite squad called the Fleet Marine Force Basketball Team. After the war, he played professionally with Oshkosh of the National Basketball League and with the Hammond Indians. In 1948, he played with the Indianapolis Jets of the NBA. He appeared in one game, scored no points, and had one assist. After the season, he came back to Texas and spent the rest of his life on his North Texas ranch.

10. "Sports of the Times: They Come Tall From Texas," *New York Times*, January 20, 1942.

11. "As I was Saying by Bob Ingram," *El Paso Herald-Post*, February 26, 1942.

12. "Here's the Dope," *Galveston Daily News*, January 24, 1942. By its very theatrical nature, basketball attracts colorful characters to its coaching ranks—none more unconventional and intriguing than Mose Simms.

John Clark Simms, born in Moody, Texas, was a rebel promoter with a big heart and a mouth that never stopped moving. He was either an evangelist or a snake oil salesman, take your pick. In addition to coaching, he ran a shoeshine stand and a hamburger joint. He was a newspaper publisher, a correspondent assigned to the inauguration of President Herbert Hoover, a radio announcer, and a successful oilman.

He promoted various high school and college all-star football and basketball games, running afoul of the University Interscholastic League and the National Collegiate Athletic Association (NCAA) in the process. Those organizations seemed to think Simms was exploiting the youth of America with his schemes and tried to put him out of business, but he always found ways to circumvent their regulations.

When the NCAA ordered a 1-year loss of college eligibility for high school graduates who participated in an all-star contest unless an appropriate state organization approved the game, Simms simply moved the date of his high school all-star game ahead of graduation.

Later Simms moved to Oklahoma where, backed by a group of businessmen, he organized the Wigwam-Wisemen of America for the advancement of sports in Oklahoma and to sponsor and underwrite his all-star contests. Officially, he was the secretary-treasurer of the organization. In reality, he *was* the organization.

Despite allegations to the contrary, Simms demonstrated repeatedly that he was not interested in making money or exploiting anyone. In fact, most of his contests lost money, leaving him to square the accounts out of his own pocket. He was in it for fun, and if his contest turned a profit, he plowed every penny back into his charitable causes.

He had a deeper love for youth than any of the organizations with which he battled. With his oil money and his charitable endeavors, he put at least one hundred boys through college and helped countless others achieve a higher education.

In October 1962, Mose Simms had a heart attack while at work in Oklahoma City. He drove himself to the hospital and walked into the emergency room. Fifteen minutes later, he died.

Chapter 4

1. Metz Lafollette played minor league baseball (1947–50) for Amarillo, Lufkin, and Lubbock. He was the head basketball coach at West Texas State from 1959 to 1962.

2. "Tall Team to Continue Tall," *The Canyon News*, October 15, 1942. After the war, Ray Ellefson played at Oklahoma A&M and at the University of Colorado. He had a 4-year career in the BAA and the NBA (1948–51) with the Minneapolis Lakers and the New York Knicks.

3. "Miller Thinks His Frosh Best Ever," *Abilene Reporter News*, March 25, 1943.

4. "Shoes Only Giants Could Fill," *The* (Hagerstown, Maryland) *Morning Herald*, January 3, 1944.

5. "Do You Want a Good Baseball Team?—Just Roll Up a Truck and Take 'Em," *San Antonio Express*, March 16, 1943.

6. "Tech Bulldogs Lose to Selman Field 13-6 in Saturday's Game," *Ruston* (Louisiana) *Daily Leader*, October 2, 1944.

7. "Few Days Off for Athletes at Carolina," *Burlington* (North Carolina) *Daily Times-News*, December 22, 1943.

8. L. Louise Box, interview.

9. "Practice Opens for WTS Cagers," *Amarillo Daily News*, October 5, 1946. See also "Plains Students Move Right in at WTSC as Barracks and Trailer Town Aid in Housing," *Amarillo Daily News*, October 5, 1946.

10. L. Louise Box, interview.

Chapter 5

1. "Basketball First Love, But Box Wowed 'Em as End for Pro Lions," *Fort Worth Star Telegram*, January 29, 1961.

2. "Story-Book Touch Behind Box's Rise to Fame," *Detroit Free Press*, August 30, 1953.

3. "Ex-football Star Cloyce Box Dies." *Dallas Morning News*, October 27, 1993.

4. Jack Curtice later coached at Utah and at Stanford. In addition to his talents as a football coach, Jack Curtice had a flair for music. He wrote the West Texas State fight song, "On, on Buffaloes."

5. "Between You and Me," *Amarillo Daily News*, October 18, 1946.

6. "Former Rockets Give Tech Scare Saturday," *Wellington* (Texas) *Leader*, September 26, 1946.

7. "Between You and Me."

8. "Nicklaus Quits and Van Meter Fired in Athletic Shakeup," *El Paso Herald-Post*, October 22, 1946.

9. "Kranzberries," *Amarillo Daily News*, November 23, 1960.

10. "West Texas Players Want to Come to Mines," *El Paso Herald-Post*, October 22, 1946.

11. "Frank Kimbrough," *Amarillo Globe-News Sunday*, March 26, 2000.

12. "West Texas Buffs Rampage Over ACC Wildcats, 41-19," *Amarillo Daily News*, September 26, 1948.

13. "Ex-football Star Cloyce Box Dies."

14. "Basketball First Love, But Box Wowed 'Em as End for Pro Lions."

15. "Story-Book Touch Behind Box's Rise to Fame."

16. "Basketball First Love, But Box Wowed 'Em as End for Pro Lions."

17. "Sports: Frank A. Godsoe," *Amarillo Daily News*, April 23, 1965.

18. "The Double Take," *Abilene Reporter-News*, December 23, 1962.

19. Tom Box, interview, August 6, 2012.

20. Doug Box, interview, August 5, 2013.

Chapter 6

1. "Ex-football Star Cloyce Box Dies."

2. "Cage Snafu Made Grid Star of Box," *Detroit Free Press*, September 30, 1953.

3. "Lions Sign Nemeth and Box," *New York Times*, June 5, 1949.

4. "Basketball First Love, But Box Wowed 'Em as End for Pro Lions."

5. "Cage Snafu Made Grid Star of Box."

6. "Basketball First Love, But Box Wowed 'Em as End for Pro Lions."

7. "Detroit conquers Baltimore, 45 to 2, Box Catches Four Touchdown Passes—Layne Completes 16 of 27—Walker Shines." *New York Times*, December 4, 1950.

8. "Voice of the Peebles," *San Antonio Express*, September 5, 1951.

9 "Ex-football Star Cloyce Box Dies."

10. "Box, Former Lion, Succumbs," *Ironwood* (Michigan) *Daily Globe*, October 26, 1993.

11. Ibid.

12. Frank Gifford, interview with the author, October 1, 2012.

13. "Walker, Layne Began Grid Play as Guards," *Mansfield* (Ohio) *News-Journal*, September 5, 1954.

14. Bill Little, Texas Sports.com, December 10, 2011.

15. "Layne Will Be Remembered as a Player Who Did It His Way," *Galveston Daily News*, December 3, 1986.
16. "Layne Lived Hard on and off the Field," *Madison* (Wisconsin) *Capital Times*, December 3, 1986.
17. "The Night Train Stops at Canton: The Nickname," *New York Times*, February 7, 1974.
18. "Tough Guys Still in Pro Football," *The Yuma* (Arizona) *Daily Sun*, November 6, 1995.
19. "Layne Lived Hard on and off the Field."
20. Tom Box, interview, August 6, 2012.

Chapter 7

1. "Grid Lions Put Skids Under Bo McMillin," *Montana Standard*, January 5, 1951.
2. "Lions' Player Revolt Figured in McMillin Firing," *Cedar Rapids* (Iowa) *Gazette*, December 27, 1950.
3. Gifford, interview.
4. "Bobby Layne Reportedly Objected to Handling of Lions by McMillin," *Lubbock Morning News*, January 5, 1951.
5. "Lions' Player Revolt Figured in McMillin Firing."
6. "Don't Like Bo," *Salt Lake Tribune*, January 5, 1951.
7. "Reveal Three Lions Stars Refuse to Play Under Bo," *Long Beach* (California) *Independent*, January 5, 1951.
8. "Once Over Lightly," *Long Beach* (California) *Independent*, January 2, 1951.
9. "Looking 'Em Over, with Tommy Hart," *Big Spring* (Texas) *Daily Herald*, January 31, 1951.
10. "Lions Owe Win to Cloyce Box," *Ludington* (Michigan) *Daily News*, October 20, 1952.
11. "Lions Silence Boos as Cloyce Box's Pass Catching Beats Rams," *The News Palladium* (Benton Harbor, Michigan), October 20, 1952.
12. Ibid.
13. Ibid.
14. "Keeping Posted with Bill Reddy," *The Post Standard* (Syracuse), August 22, 1953.
15. "Loss of One Man Bothers LA Ram Coach No Little," *The Humboldt Times* (Eureka, California), December 19, 1952.
16. "Article 4, No Title," *New York Times*, December 18, 1952.
17. "Win Division Playoff Over Rams, 31-21," *The News-Palladium* (Benton Harbor, Michigan), December 22, 1952.
18. "Line and Box Get Credit in Clam Clubhouse After Lions Attain First Crown in 17 Years," *New York Times*, December 29, 1952.
19. Ibid., "Lions Get 5 Berths on All-Pro Eleven," *New York Times*, January 9, 1953,
20. "The Scoreboard," *Gastonia* (North Carolina) *Gazette*, July 30, 1966.

Chapter 8

1. "Kerbawy Texas Roundup," *Racine* (Wisconsin) *Journal Times*, February 26, 1953.

2. "Layne Signs Pact with Detroit Club," *Odessa* (Texas) *American*, February 26, 1953. See also "Time Out with Maurice Smith," *Winnipeg Free Press*, June 14, 1952.

3. "College All-Stars Have a Lot To Learn," *St. Joseph* (Michigan) *Herald Press*, August 15, 1953.

4. "College All-Stars Have Lots To Learn Before They Can Rank With Pros," *Long Beach* (California) *Press-Telegram*, August 15, 1953.

5. "Basketball First Love, But Box Wowed 'Em as End for Pro Lions."

6. "In the Huddle," *Pacific Stars and Stripes*, November 21, 1966.

7. Ibid., "Grid Lions Sign Parker for '54: Predicts Third Straight Title," *European Stars and Stripes*, January 24, 1954.

8. "Doak May Hang Up Cleats for Good," *San Antonio Express*, April 7, 1955.

9. "Detroit Coach Predicts Lions, Browns Win Again," *Bakersfield Californian*, January 5, 1955.

10. Gifford, interview.

Chapter 9

1. Frank Cannon's brother was the actor J. D. Cannon who played Chief Peter B. Clifford in *McCloud*, Harry Briscoe in *Alias Smith and Jones*, and Society Red in *Cool Hand Luke*. J. D. Cannon also played the witness who cleared Dr. Richard Kimble in the final episode of *The Fugitive*.

2. "Picture—Caption," *The Van Nuys* (California) *News*, January 13, 1955, 4C.

3. "Soundtrack," *Sports Illustrated*, September 10, 1954.

4. Ibid.

5. Ibid.

6. Maurice Campbell, interview with the author, August 25, 2009.

7. Kent Hance, interview with the author, October 20, 2016.

8. Norman Smith, interview with the author, October 24, 2016.

9. Tom Box, interview, August 6, 2012.

10. Gifford, interview.

11. Campbell, interview.

12. Doug Box, interview, October 12, 2012.

13. Campbell, interview, August 25, 2009.

14. Tom Box, interview, August 6, 2012. "I first met John Wayne in the 1940s," Frank Gifford explained. "USC got me a part-time job as an extra in the movies. It was a great recruiting tool. That's where I first met John Wayne." From an interview with Frank Gifford, October 1, 2012.

15. Ibid.

16. Gifford, interview.

17. Hugh Aynesworth, interview with the author, November 2, 2013.

18. Billy Dyer, interview with the author, April 18, 2012.
19. Blake Lovelace Jr., interview with the author, April 2, 2013.
20. Smith, interview, October 24, 2016.
21. Wilmuth Box-Johnson, letter.
22. Doug Box, interview, October 12, 2012.

Chapter 10

1."Valero's Success Sprang Out of Troubles; Suits, SpinoffsTthen; Fortune Top 10 Now," *San Antonio Express-News,* May 12, 2013. On January 1, 1980, Lovaca Gathering Company became Valero Energy Corporation. Today, Valero is a Fortune 500 company.

2. "World Owes Carter Its Thanks," *Indiana Gazette,* October 1, 1994.

3. "Document Implies Texas Oil Man Conspired with Iraqi Government," *Elyria* (Ohio) *Chronicle-Telegram,* August 18, 2007.

4. Tom Box, interview, August 6, 2012.

5. Gary Adams, interview with the author, September 2, 2016.

6. Tom Box, interview, August 6, 2012.

7. David Ownby, interview with the author, August 24, 2016.

8. The house is gone, but if you walk a short distance and look east, you will see two of Crow's magnificent monuments: Bryan Tower and Trammell Crow Center.

9. William Bragg Ewald, Jr., *Trammell Crow: A Legacy of Real Estate Innovation* (Washington, DC: The Urban Land Institute, 2005).

10. Tom Box, interview, August 6, 2012.

11. Maurice Campbell, interview, August 29, 2009.

12. W. O. Bankston, the legendary Dallas businessman and car dealer, was born in Winters, Texas in 1913. Within a year of his birth, the family had moved to Brownwood.

Bankston's father had a broken back and couldn't work. The family lived in poverty. Bankston went to work on a milk truck at age six to help care for his family including two younger brothers. His formal education was over in the sixth grade.

During the Depression, he rode a boxcar from Brownwood to Dallas. He arrived in "Big D" with a dollar in his pocket.

He worked as an embalmer's assistant and on the assembly line at the Ford plant. He began selling cars in 1934. He schmoozed his way into a partnership in a used car lot in 1937. In 1941, bankrolled by oilman G. E. Hall, Bankston bought a Ford dealership and launched Bankston-Hall Motors, Inc.

Ford couldn't build cars fast enough for W. O. Bankston. He could sell sand in West Texas. For 2 years, he pre-sold cars yet to be built.

To boost sales even more, he sometimes sponsored stag parties to entertain buyers. The star of the shows was famed stripper Juanita Dale Slusher, better known as Candy Barr. Bankston met Candy at Barney Weinstein's Colony Club, two doors down from Jack Ruby's Carousel Club on Commerce Street in downtown Dallas. Candy was friends with Jack Ruby, and she was the connection between Bankston and Ruby that fueled rumors of Bankston's role in the Kennedy assassination.

Bankston loved sports. He was a partner in several minor league baseball teams. He made an offer to buy the Minneapolis Lakers, but the franchise moved to Los Angeles. He and a group of financiers tried to buy the Dallas Cowboys in 1984.

He and two other Dallas businessmen once bought 5,000 tickets to lift the blackout of a Dallas Cowboys playoff game so Bankston's daughter, who had multiple sclerosis, could watch the contest on television. He gave the tickets away for free at his dealerships.

13. Ewald, *Trammell Crow*, 103.

14. "Touch of Class: 38 Years Ago, Future Hall of Famers, President-to-Be Met on Football Field," *Dallas Morning News*, January 15, 1989.

15. Ibid.

16. Tom Box, interview with the author, September 2, 2016.

17. "Spalding Sells Rawlings Unit to a Group of Noted Investors." *New York Times*, September 5, 1963.

18. "Frank A. Godsoe," *Amarillo Sunday News-Globe*, August 17, 1967.

19. Ibid.

20. "Regent Resigns WTSU Post," *Dallas Morning News*, March 24, 1973.

Chapter 11

1. Doug Box, interview, October 12, 2012.

2. Moore's boss in the early years was Fred Smith whose son, Fred Smith Jr., founded FedEx.

3. "George A. Fuller Approves an Offer for Private Ownership." *New York Times*, April 7, 1965.

4. "George A. Fuller Co. Holders to Vote Today On Plan to 'Go Private,'" *Wall Street Journal*, June 7, 1965.

5. Tom Box, interview, August 6, 2012.

6. "George A. Fuller Co. Holders to Vote Today On Plan to 'Go Private.'"

7. *New York Times*, June 8, 1965, "Fuller Becoming Private Company," p59, c3.

8. Ibid.

9. Ibid.

10. "Holders of George A. Fuller Vote in Favor of Management Proposal to 'Go Private.'"

11. Ibid. See also "Fuller Becoming Private Company: Meeting of Publically Owned Concern Supports Sale Despite Opposition," *New York Times*, June 8, 1965.

12. Ewald, *Trammell Crow*, 104.

13. Ibid.

14. Doug Box, interview, October 12, 2012

15. Ewald, *Trammell Crow*.

16. Doug Box, interview, October 12, 2012.

17. Wilmuth Box-Johnson, letter.

18. "Jet Lands Here," *Ruston* (Louisiana) *Daily Leader*, October 14, 1971.
19. Maurice Campbell, interview, August 25, 2009.
20. Doug Box, interview.
21. Frank Gifford, interview.
22. David Ownby, interview.
23. Doug Box, interview, October 12, 2012.

Chapter 12

1. Doug Box, interview, October 12, 2012.
2. Ibid. At one point in its existence, the president of OKC Corp was D. W. Rentzel, the father of Dallas Cowboys star Lance Rentzel. See "OKC President Quits for 'Other' Interests," *Wall Street Journal*, May 9, 1969.
3. Andrew Sansom, "The Friends of Cloyce Box," *Texas Monthly*, December 1978.
4. Doug Box, interview, October 12, 2012.
5. "$12 Million Cement Plant at New Orleans," *Biloxi Daily Herald*, December 14, 1962.
6. "Touch of Class."
7. "Mergers," *Lowell* (Massachusetts) *Sun*, July 16, 1969.
8. OKC v. FTC, 455 F.2d 1159 (10th Cir. Court, 1972).
9. "Sale Ordered," *The San Antonio Express/News*, October 24, 1970.
10. *OKC*, 455 F.2d 1159.
11. "Ex-football Star Cloyce Box Dies."
12. Sansom, "Friends of Cloyce Box."
13. Doug Box, interview, October 12, 2012.

Chapter 13

1. "Oklahoma Cement Buys Phillips Petroleum Co. in Oklahoma," *Wall Street Journal*, November 1, 1966.
2. Sansom, "Friends of Cloyce Box."
3. Ibid.
4. "Texas Cover-Up: Why Did OKC Chief Conceal His Oil Sales to Friendly Brokers?" *Wall Street Journal*, May 13, 1980. See also "Firm Fined $5.25 Million," *Brownsville Herald*, July 20, 1980.
5. Sansom, "Friends of Cloyce Box."
6. "Texas Judge Orders an Article Delayed," *Wall Street Journal*, May 11, 1980.
7. "Firm Fined $5.25 Million."
8. "Resisting the SEC, Texas-Style," *New York Times*, August 21, 1979.
9. "SEC Cites Kickbacks at OKC," *New York Times*, September 16, 1980.
10. Sansom, "Friends of Cloyce Box."
11. "Texas Cover-Up."
12. Doug Box, interview, August 5, 2013.
13. Gary Adams, interview with the author, September 27, 2016.
14. "Texas Cover-Up."
15. Ibid.

16. Gary Adams, interview, September 27, 2016.
17. OKC Corp. v. Harold M. Williams, 490 F. Supp. 560 (N.D. Tex. 1979).
18. "Resisting the SEC, Texas-Style."
19. "Texas Cover-Up."
20. Ibid.
21. "Resisting the SEC, Texas-Style."
22. Sansom, "Friends of Cloyce Box."
23. Ibid.
24. Stephen G. Michaud, "A Lawyer Who Can Tie the SEC in Knots," *Texas Business*, December 1980, 21.
25. Sansom, "Friends of Cloyce Box."
26. Gary Adams, interview, September 27, 2016.
27. "Texas Cover-Up."
28. Sansom, "Friends of Cloyce Box."
29. Norman Smith, interview with the author, October 25, 2016.
30. "Texas Cover-Up."
31. Department of Justice to Cloyce K. Box, memorandum, July 17, 1980.
32. "Firm Fined $5.25 Million." See also "Corporation Head Accused by SEC of Kickbacks Scheme," *Colorado Springs Gazette*, September 16, 1980.
33. "OKC Penalties Set in Oil Pricing Case," *New York Times*, July 18, 1980.
34. "OKC Reaches S.E.C. Accord," *New York Times*, December 18, 1980. See also "Fit to Be Fried," *Texas Observer*, May 11, 1995.
35. Ibid.
36. "Complaint Names Cloyce K. Box and OKC Corp.," *SEC News Digest* 80–184 (September 19, 1980).
37. "Corporation Head Accused by SEC of Kickbacks Scheme."
38. SEC v. Cloyce K. Box and OKC Corp., Civil Action No. 3-80-12170 (N.D. Tex. 1980). See also "Complaint Names Cloyce K. Box and OKC Corp."
39. Ibid.
40. Maurice Campbell, interview with the author, August 25, 2009.
41. Ibid.
42. Ibid.

Chapter 14

1. "Texas Cover-Up."
2. "Stockholders of OKC Vote to Liquidate Firm," *Paris* (Texas) *News*, May 14, 1980.
3. Michaud, "Knots," 25.
4. *OKC Corp.*, 490 F. Supp. 560. See also "Texas Judge Orders an Article Delayed."
5. "Texas Judge Orders an Article Delayed."
6. "News Suppression Foiled," *Cedar Rapids* (Iowa) *Gazette*, May 16, 1980.
7. "Wall Street Journal Told to Hold Story on Oil Firm," *The Sunday Sun* (Lowell, Massachusetts), May 11, 1980.
8. "News Suppression Foiled."

9. Sansom, "Friends of Cloyce Box."

10. "Texas Cover-Up."

11. Ibid.

12. "Liquidation Vote 400-1," *Colorado Springs Gazette Telegraph*, May 14, 1980. See also "OKC to Be Disbanded, Chairman Linked to Scandal," *The Stars and Stripes*, May 15, 1980.

13. "Saudis Get Favored Treatment," *Roswell* (New Mexico) *Daily Record*, July 23, 1978.

14. "Resisting the SEC, Texas-Style." See also "Pharaon Considering making OKC Offer," *New York Times*, June 7, 1978. Several years earlier, Pharaon was implicated in the infamous BCCI (Bank of Credit and Commerce International) scandal, the same scandal that caused the resignation of Bert Lance, President Jimmy Carter's Director of the Office of Budget and Management. BCCI, founded by a Pakistani financier and at one time the seventh largest private bank in the world, was involved in money laundering and all kinds of dirty deeds. Pharaon got involved in US banking when he bought shares in The National Bank of Georgia from Lance. Pharaon was also a major investor in Harken Energy, future President George W. Bush's first business venture. BCCI once gave Harken Energy a $25 million emergency loan. Pharaon and his partner, Abdullah Bakhsh, sat on Harken's board of directors. Bakhsh's banker, Khalid bin Mahfouz, also owned shares of Harken Energy he inherited from his kinsman, Salem bin Laden, the half-brother and cousin of Osama bin Laden.

15. "Texas Cover-Up."

16. Ibid.

17. Michaud, "Knots," 22.

18. "Resisting the SEC, Texas-Style."

19. Ibid.

20. Michaud, "Knots," 25.

21. "OKC Ex-Chairman Ends 5 Year-Old SEC Lawsuit," *Dallas Morning News*, September 21, 1984.

22. Michaud, "Knots," 25.

23. Ibid

24. Gary Adams, interview, September 27, 2016.

25. Ibid.

26. David Ownby, interview.

27. "Receiver Appointed for Refinery," *The Paris* (Texas) *News*, June 7, 1981.

28. "Firm Fined $5.25 Million."

29. "OKC Corp. Looking for Fuel Partners," *New York Times*, February 28, 1981.

30. B. R. Griffin, et al., v. Thomas D. Box and Don D. Box, Independent Co-Executors of the Estate of Cloyce K.

31. Ibid.

32. "Box Energy Feud Ends; Purchase Expected," *Dallas Morning News*, August 30, 1997.

33. Doug Box, interview, August 5, 2013.

34. Ibid.

35. "Fit to Be Fried," *Dallas Observer*, May 11, 1995. See also "Wall Street; A Tangled Web Called Box Energy," *New York Times*, January 2, 1994.

Chapter 15

1. Phillips Oil Company v. OKC Corp., 812 F.2d 265 (5th Cir. 1987).
2. "Ex-football Star Cloyce Box Dies."
3. *Phillips Oil Company*, 812 F.2d 265.
4. *Griffin*. 85 F.3d 625.
5. *Phillips Oil Company*, 812 F.2d 265.
6. Kent Hance, interview.
7. Ibid.
8. Norman Smith, interview with the author, October 25, 2016.
9. "Fit to Be Fried."
10. Ibid.
11. According to the *New York Times*, June 30, 2012, Delaware is a corporate haven—a rival to the Cayman Islands. Companies that shift their royalties to holding companies in Delaware are not taxed, regardless of where they do business. Nearly half of all public corporations in the United States are incorporated in Delaware.
12. "Wall Street: A Tangled Web Called Box Energy," *New York Times*, June 2, 1994.
13. "Fit to Be Fried."
14. Ibid.
15. "Market Place: A Texas Case Tests the Limits of Director's Responsibilities," *New York Times*, July 19, 1980.
16. "Box Energy Ruling Could Redefine Directors' Roles," *Dallas Morning News*, July 19, 1993.
17. Ibid.
18. "Fit to Be Fried."
19. "Box Energy Feud Ends; Purchase Expected," *Dallas Morning News*, August 30, 1997. See also "Fit to Be Fried.
20. "Wall Street."
21. Maurice Campbell, interview, August 25, 2009.
22. "The No Funds League," *Los Angeles Times*, July 29, 2000.
23. Maurice Campbell, interview, August 25, 2009.
24. Governor John Y. Brown Jr., interview with the author, November 23, 2013.
25. Yale Lary, interview with the author, October 14, 2013.
26. David Ownby, interview.
27. Hugh Aynesworth, interview.

Chapter 16

1. Doug Box, interview, February 2, 2009.
2. Ibid.
3. Fern married Charles C. Carr, a retired air force pilot, in 1991. He died in 2006. Fern died of a stroke on September 4, 2007. She is buried in Harp Cemetery in Arkansas.

4. Doug Box, interview, February 2, 2009.

5. Ibid.

6. Tom Box, interview, August 6, 2012.

7. "Dallas Part Is Broadening," *Burlington* (North Carolina) *Times-News*, November 4, 1978.

8. Tom Box, interview, August 6, 2012.

9. Alan Peppard, dallasnews.com, June 8, 2012.

10. "What They Think of 'Dallas' in Dallas," *New York Times*, January 9, 1980.

11. "Nobody's Slicker Than Jack," *Dallas Morning News*, April 29, 1992.

Chapter 17

1. Maurice Campbell, interview, August 25, 2009.

2. Doug Box, interview, October 12, 2012.

3. "Mexicans Dumping Cheap Cement in US," *Kingston* (Jamaica) *Gleaner*, July 13, 1990.

4. "TXI Permit Hearings Begin Monday at Duncanville Holiday Inn," *Duncanville Today*, February 5, 1988.

5. "Cement Makers Fault Mexicans," *New York Times*, September 28, 1989.

6. "Focus: Overbuilding Developers; Redirecting Energies," *New York Times*, June 5, 1988.

7. "Trammell Crow, Alive but Humbled," *New York Times*, August 30, 1983.

8. Doug Box, interview, October 12, 2012.

9. Maurice Campbell, interview, August 25, 2009.

10. "Box Crow Cement Files for Chapter 11," *The Dallas Morning News*, August 5, 1992.

11. "Midlothian, Box-Crow Cement Changes Hands," *Duncanville Standard*, June 15, 1989.

12. "Midlothian's Holcim Seeks Community Respect," *Duncanville Progress*, January 30, 2003. See also "Crow Family, Swiss Company Buy Midlothian Cement Plant," *Dallas Morning News*, May 29, 1993.

13. "Crow Family, Swiss Company Buy Midlothian Cement Plant."

14. Doug Box, interview, October 12, 2012.

15. Ibid.

Index